THE HEALING OF MY
SOUL

THE HEALING OF MY SOUL

The Psychotherapy of an Incest Survivor

LEIA HUGHEY Ph. D.

ARPress
ILLUMINATING IDEAS.
EMPOWERING VOICES

ARPress
45 Dan Road Suite 5
Canton MA 02021

Hotline:	1(888) 821-0229
Fax:	1(508) 545-7580

Ordering Information:

Quantity sales. Special discounts are available on quantity purchases by corporations, associations, and others. For details, contact the publisher at the address above.

Printed in the United States of America.

ISBN-13:	Softcover	979-8-89330-340-7
	eBook	979-8-89330-342-1

Library of Congress Control Number: 2024900955

The Healing of My Soul by Leia Hughey, Ph.D.

Many, many years before Bessel van der Kolk described the myriad ways in which The Body Keeps the Score, Leia Hughey had already embarked on a process of interpreting her physical symptoms, deciphering messages from her dreams, and listening to her most deeply held intuitive wisdom to expose, heal, and even reach closure around one of the most horrifyingly violent acts a young child can ever experience. In The Healing of My Soul: The Psychotherapy of an Incest Survivor, Leia shares the incredibly personal details of her process of discovering her own childhood rape and, importantly, for those who may share similar histories, describes the intricacies of the therapeutic approaches she engaged in and how each played a part in her ability to heal. There is now a rapidly growing body of research that not only fully supports her methods but is also beginning to document the means through which more wholistic (inclusive of body, mind, and spirit) therapies work. This book reads like a stay-up-late-because-you-can't-possibly-put-it-down mystery but should be a required textbook for college students in a wide array of majors, not just psychology. My wish is that this book lands in the hands of anyone who has experienced childhood trauma or, most especially, those who work with them in any kind of professional capacity or interact with them in an intimate sense. This is the awareness that we need and the process we must individually and collectively go through if we have any hope of developing more safe, sane, and sustainable communities. Leia's writing is nearly as exquisite as her soul. She describes events and dynamics that would otherwise be deemed unspeakable, putting them so eloquently into words that not only penetrate, but ultimately soothe and cure. Through sharing the experiences of her younger selves—often from journal entries written at the time—Leia acts as a compassionate guide for anyone who longs to pursue their own healing journey. The path is made much, much clearer in these pages.

Nita Halstead, MCoun
School Counselor
Eugene, OR

Contents

Acknowledgements

I am not exaggerating when I say that the re-release of this book would not have happened without the surprising enthusiasm and encouragement of my editor, Nita Halstead. I knew Nita as a member of our community who had a personal interest in childhood sexual abuse. Although I did not know her especially well, I trusted her on the basis of what I did know and I asked her to review the book for the possibility of releasing it for a second time. In our very first conversation she convinced me that the book had a destiny and purpose beyond what I was currently entertaining. Nita has a passion for purposeful cultural change. Her optimism that meaningful transformation is possible is utterly contagious.

The therapists who worked with me during those years were essentially shooting in the dark as was I. We were on a journey without a clear understanding of the destination. I am forever grateful to Charles P. Cummings, Ph.D., Morgan Worthy, Ph.D. and Edward W. Smith, Ph.D. The work each one did with me was proof positive that therapy can open doors. My family was wonderful during the years of my recovery. I extend special recognition to my sister, Judy, who patiently listened hour after hour of my outpouring of grief and questioning my own sanity. I know she had to have wondered if my languishing in my personal despair would ever end. Her life was also touched by pedophilia when her children were molested by a family member. We bonded together trying to come to terms with the sometimes harsh realities of life. We kept each other focused on healing.

My brother, the late James A. Hanson, had a way of interjecting balance through humor. I have a tendency to be serious to a fault. On the occasion that I informed him that I realized I'd been molested as a little girl, he fell silent for a moment then blurted, "Was it me?" His response so violated my expectations that I could not restrain my laughter. I don't think he realized how important his playfulness in the face of trauma was for me. His irreverence contained the seeds of my coming to realize this didn't need to be a tragedy. I envy heaven where I am certain he is entertaining others endlessly with his unique and quirky sense of humor. May his joy and laughter fill the universe!

Jack is at the center of this book. The actions he took intending for the fulfillment of sexual deviancy will be put to the purpose of healing others. I will always wonder who Jack was, in his right thinking mind.

Preface

When *The Healing of My Soul* was first released in the early 1990's it was amidst the debate as to whether the outpouring of sexual abuse stories was legitimate. The coining of the term "false memory syndrome" took place and lawsuits with high financial settlements at stake made media headlines. The book you are now reading was displayed on a national television news program as an example of the multitude of books that were being written by sexual abuse survivors. The word "epidemic" was used by commentators to describe the, then recent, flood of what was often referred to as "alleged incest victims". Research psychologists everywhere seized the momentum of the roiling debate to study properties of memory with the underlying question being whether the flood of sexual abuse allegations could be true. While that debate was in full swing, reports of sexual abuse of nearly every variety was on a steady rise. The paradox was mind boggling to observe. Those accused of being predators were aggressively trying to silence their accusers and prove their innocence by casting doubt on the claims made against them.

While there may have been complex motives on the part of prosecutors and defendants for settling these cases, the net result of all the uncertainty and confusion was that it effectively drained energy away from treating and healing survivors of this type of intimate betrayal. I recall attending a professional meeting in which a colleague confessed in a public setting of similarly trained professionals that he had abandoned the practice of routinely inquiring of the client whether he or she had any knowledge of having been sexually abused. Lawsuits against psychologists who were treating sexual abuse survivors began making the headlines and the profession at large was pulled into the fray. Fear about broaching the subject with clients permeated the helping professions. I personally felt pressed between my own firsthand experience of repressed memory plus the influence it had on my global development and the emerging social opinion of disbelief and invalidation that was building. I was among the fortunate with survivors in that I had confirmation and validation that the abuse had occurred and I wasn't merely seeking dramatic attention. Many other survivors of abuse who had developed their personality and emotional patterns around the traumatic events had no such validation and now faced social pressure to put any awareness of the possibility of such a thing soundly out of their mind.

One personal example of how the social debate was being acted out by health practitioners might be illustrative. Shortly after this book was first released, I recall having gone for a therapeutic massage with a licensed massage therapist while attending a training conference. I had given the therapist information about my background, including the rape as part of the routine intake paperwork. To my astonishment, while I was undergoing my massage for my relaxation and tension release, the therapist entered into a steady stream of monologue discounting my trauma experience, basically suggesting to me that I was delusional, and that the rape had been imagined. Since I already had confirming evidence of the childhood experience, I was perplexed by the opinion proffered by the massage therapist. The therapist was no doubt expressing the building popularity of the notion that sexual abuse reports represented a type of mass hysteria. The idea that anyone seeking treatment to recover from sexual trauma was suffering from "false memory syndrome" had proved to be a convenient tool for treatment providers to participate in the cultural denial of what was happening, and had happened to untold numbers of children everywhere and across time.

It is not the purpose this book to reopen the memory debates. Errors can be made in either direction. It is well established that memory details can be moving targets. A large measure of common sense is a necessity when assessing sexual abuse reports. A very positive contribution of the controversy over "false memory" was that conversations opened up about context of the hidden abuse of children. The *context* of the experiences is of paramount importance to consider for accuracy, and even more so for healing. The controversy provided the impetus to study sexual predators and the lasting effects of abuse including the effects of trauma on the brain and on memory. More good than harm was gleaned from that social conversation.

The purpose of this book is to chronicle a healing process that was founded upon injury held in repressed memory, the details of which were fleshed out across a span of more than a decade. While it is my own story, my healing process highlights universal elements of recovery that will resonate with survivors and be instructive to readers with any level of interest. With the debates over memory having waned as a distraction, it is my genuine hope that this story will encourage the redirecting of available resources and energy toward understanding and *healing* both perpetrators as well as those harmed.

Introduction

Leia has done a remarkably brave thing by going public. She has taken some of her most private and painful experiences and put them in written form to be read by all who will. This is a particularly brave act, for Leia not only has dredged up such excruciating and crazy-making material from her depths, but she has set this material afloat in the waters of public domain. Once cast afloat, Leia has no control over how the material will be received, understood or misunderstood, valued or depreciated. My hope and request is that you, the readers, will handle this material with the respect that it and Leia deserve, learning from it what you can.

When Leia called me and told me of her project and asked that I contribute my perspective on her therapy, I agreed with enthusiasm. Later I thought long and hard about my decision. Psychotherapy is such a private matter. Although there are notable exceptions, the tradition from Freud's time on has been to protect confidentiality by keeping therapy very private. The assurance of confidentiality is one of the ways to make the therapy session safe enough to encourage deep intrapersonal exploration and full-blown authentic emotional expression. Leia has chosen to open the closed door of the consulting room. I accept her wishes, as I have before, respecting her right and her clearness of judgment. But this project also means my discussing the rationale and style of my therapy with Leia. The actual sessions were not recorded, so we cannot offer any verbatim account. In addition, I decided that I was not interested in writing any lengthy theoretical essay on psychotherapy or on the treatment of survivors of childhood sexual abuse in general. My theoretical statement on psychotherapy was sufficiently fresh that I would let it stand as written in *The Body In Psychotherapy* (Smith, 2007).

-Edward W.L. Smith, Ph.D.

1
CHAPTER

The cornerstone of every successful therapeutic encounter, regardless of theoretical orientation of the therapist or beliefs of the client, is trust. Every therapist knows or has been taught at some point that no matter how skilled he or she may be, therapy will go nowhere without the formation of a trusting connection between the therapist and the client.

When I embarked upon my first personal therapy experience, I was almost devoid of trust for the mental health professions. Ironically, I was a senior in college majoring in psychology, and a registered nurse working in a psychiatric unit. My reasons for seeking therapy, so I thought, were related to my work in psychiatry. While I knew I had a history of mild chronic depression (untreated), the reason I gave for presenting to the University Counseling Center for therapy was that I wanted help in assessing my proper role in the psychiatric unit where I worked, and I had no intention of addressing the depression.

My first nursing job following graduation from nursing school at the age of twenty-three was in psychiatry. While there were many aspects of my work that seemed exciting and magical, there were other experiences that left me with doubt and insecurity about my values. I sincerely loved patient contact and my natural curiosity about the inner life of others helped me listen to those in my care with a nonjudgmental ear. What I lacked in skill and training I made up for in sincerity, goodwill, and patience. I approached work with a high level of integrity and a sense of justice and fairness, giving the best of myself to those patients in my charge. My personal standards, however, had a way of keeping me off balance with other professionals with whom my work interfaced. For example, there is a practice used in hospitals at the change of shifts called "report." I was stunned the first time I sat in on one of these meetings where the daytime and evening personnel exchanged information about the patients' progress. Staff members would describe various pathological expressions and behaviors of a patient and then make jokes about the behaviors, igniting everyone's laughter. I was torn between joining the party, or standing up and expressing righteous indignation. I believed I'd have won a reputation for being an eccentric, and I was afraid of being judged harshly by my peers. So I generally sat quietly, listened to the reports, and tolerated my discomfort. I found these meetings to be most disturbing for their cruelty. Often, the clients about whom the greatest laughter occurred were those in the greatest distress or with the most serious symptoms. It just didn't seem fair to me.

There were other observations I made of inpatient psychiatry that troubled me. It seemed that every patient admitted to the units where I'd worked was put on medication from the moment of crossing the threshold. Some benefited and were discharged quickly. However, others experienced personality changes along with other side effects like lethargy, weight gain, dry mouth, or coordination problems. Sometimes people were admitted for what seemed like normal reactions to traumatic life events. Yet they were placed on medications that I dispensed, often feeling conflict as I did so. I frequently wondered if anyone told this segment of our inpatient population that their reactions made pretty good sense in the light of their circumstances. Again, it didn't seem fair.

Not only were certain psychiatric practices disturbing for me, but so were the personal lives of the staff members. Some were heavily involved in drugs and alcohol. Some were involved in unconventional personal therapy and prided themselves in achieving "breakthroughs" of superior insight, occasionally urging patients to follow their lead. I recall feeling mildly threatened by these tales of therapy, feeling I was somehow inferior, but I didn't know why I felt as I did. Some of the staff were sexually involved with other staff members and, now and then, I heard rumors of sex with patients following hospital discharge. Worst of all, there was the backstabbing, petty jealousy, and periodic temperamental outbursts that made me extremely uncomfortable. The general behavior of the staff resembled that of a grossly dysfunctional family, with lurid secrets, excesses, and power alliances. I didn't feel safe with my coworkers and it affected my performance at times. Although I was generally considered by myself and others to be a mild person, two years in this environment was taking its toll. I was becoming irritable and unpredictable. On one occasion when two staff members argued about an admission, which neither of them wanted to write up, I slammed a chart down on the desk and declared in a loud and critical voice, "Admissions are part of the job both of you are being paid to do." Later I felt embarrassed and wondered, Am I expecting too much? Am I making unreasonable demands? I didn't trust my own perception and secretly wondered if I wasn't the person with the greatest problem. I needed help understanding and managing my occupational stress. Believing that all mental health treatment facilities would resemble my place of employment, I feared that if I sought treatment I would be treated as our staff treated patients, and I was very apprehensive.

There were other reasons, I told myself, for seeking therapy that justified challenging my own fear and entering the process. I had decided to apply to graduate school in psychology at Georgia State University, and I'd been told that the faculty gave a heavy weight in their admissions decisions to those applicants with experience working in mental health who also demonstrated a strong commitment to personal growth. Very few students had gained admission to the clinical psychology program without possessing a history that included personal therapy. A year of therapy, I reasoned, would strengthen my application, and I needed all the help I could get since competition for admission was notoriously fierce.

Armed with my justifications I was, nevertheless, intimidated by the thought of entering therapy. I didn't much like being the focus of attention or having someone else control the flow of the conversation. I was a secretive person, through no particular choosing of my own, but I seldom questioned the purpose of my secrecy. I just assumed secrecy was my style and that others weren't interested in me anyway. Looking ahead I realized that for me to become a psychotherapist, I would have a natural protection from my revealing much about myself. The focus would always be on the "other," and I would offer my compassionate support from behind my safe, protective barrier.

I convinced myself that I would be "safe" as a therapy patient because I was reasonably intelligent, facile with the language, and clear about my intentions and goals for therapy. The staff at the counseling center wasn't likely to get too many sadistic laughs from my raising questions about professional ethics, or from discussions of strategies for gaining admission to graduate school. And, I planned, I wouldn't provide enough personal information to warrant a diagnosis.

I strongly objected to giving hospital patients diagnoses because I had seen how staff therapists and psychiatrists dehumanized patients on the basis of labels. I felt fairly confident that I could avoid demonstrating those behaviors I knew to be associated with standard diagnostic criteria. I envisioned my therapy experience as perhaps a boring, academic ritual where I would go each week to discuss professional practice issues and learn a few techniques for enhancing my own skill as a therapist. Yes, I thought, this won't be too bad. I can keep it safe.

$\mathcal{2}$
CHAPTER

$\mathcal{C}$harles Cummings (Chuck) was a psychology intern finishing his doctorate at Georgia State University when I presented for therapy. I'd gone through an intake interview with another therapist and I'd felt anxious but in control. I'd been able to stay on my "professional issues" plan, and I reassured myself there was not much for me to worry about. My first meeting with Chuck was both a tremendous success and an utter disaster according to various perspectives of my consciousness. Chuck was young, as I had expected. He was tall and lean with dark hair, a beard, and dark brown eyes that seemed home to a playful twinkle. I judged him to be very handsome, and his appearance was mildly disconcerting. I would rather have been assigned to an unattractive academic type, but I could still handle this I thought. I quickly assured myself that any attraction I might be feeling was unilateral since I was certain my own appearance was quite ordinary and, besides, I was safely married. I quickly encased my immediate attraction by some reflexive internal means so that it wouldn't interfere with my plan.

We weren't far into the interview before I knew my plan was in serious trouble. I was telling him about how concerned I was about the fair treatment of hospital patients and how helpless I felt to protect them from those uncompassionate professionals entrusted with their care. Chuck responded by asking if I'd ever felt myself to be treated unfairly by those I trusted. His question caused me to personalize an experience I was trying to keep at a safe emotional distance. I answered, "Yes, I'm sure, but I don't recall anything specific. Hasn't everyone experienced injustice?" I was holding my own, I thought, deflecting perceived attacks.

Chuck kept asking me about feelings and in reply I offered thoughts and justifications, trying my best to look good. Yet I was feeling more and more threatened. Each time I offered an issue I was willing to discuss, he moved to personalize the content. Deep inside, part of me felt like I was losing a desperate battle, while another part was appreciating the pursuit and secretly hoping he would win. The encounter seemed like a contest, a test of will for me. I hated the recognition that the greater part of my conscious intent was to fool this man and keep him away. From what, I had no idea. It undermined my self-respect to admit that I really only wanted to use the available services without an honest, genuine commitment to therapy. I wanted the credit for personal growth to support my graduate school application, but I didn't want to feel threatened, vulnerable, sad, angry, or out of control in the process. Ultimately, I did not want to feel anything.

Chuck's continuous flow of personal questions eroded my defenses. He didn't seem to sense my rising anxiety, or my increasing struggle to maintain control. Emotions were moving toward the surface. He was asking me about my life, inching toward questions regarding my childhood. I could see it coming but I couldn't think of a strategically suitable way to stop this line of questioning without appearing defensive. If I was defensive, I wouldn't look good, and looking good was so important to my plan. A lump was growing in my throat, the room seemed warmer, and I was squirming in my chair. I asked for a cigarette, but he didn't smoke and I was fresh out. I wanted to bolt for the door but, more than that, I wanted to appear in control.

Could Chuck see my panic? If he did, he gave no indication. In fact, he seemed utterly casual as he fired one personal question after the next. His casual demeanor reassured me for a moment. I must be containing my panic well enough , I reasoned, because he doesn't seem to notice. Then it happened! He calmly asked, "And what about your parents?" My strategy to keep emotions at a safe distance disintegrated despite my resistance. I felt a wall collapse somewhere in my chest and unwelcome pain push its way into my consciousness. Burning tears began streaming down my face; I instantly felt both angry and ashamed as I responded, "What do my parents have to do with anything?" knowing full well that the question was absurd, given my tears. I felt like a prideful child just caught in a lie. Chuck responded by saying exactly what I was thinking: "Well, it appears they have to do with everything." His voice softened, the questions stopped, and there I sat, with my shame and uncontrolled tears, feeling conspicuous and unprotected, so alone and vulnerable.

I rarely discussed my childhood with anyone and felt disloyal and guilty if I did. As a young child, my mother had taught me that children who spoke ill of their parents were low class and generally bad. She directed me to have nothing to do with anyone who disparaged his or her parents. The message was clear: if I ever spoke of anything uncomplimentary about my parents I, too, would be low class and bad. I was naturally loyal to them, but I was also a psychological hostage as a result of my not wanting to fall into low-class status, as my mother told me I would if I didn't follow her instructions.

I left Chuck's office when my time was up, struggling to compose myself, to re-contain my sadness, my embarrassment, and what I viewed as my defeat. Before leaving, I reassured Chuck that I would be all right. I agreed to return the following week.

Driving home, I envisioned a staff meeting at the counseling center where Chuck would present my "case" and the staff would find hilarity in my naiveté about the role of my history in my present struggles. "Imagine a psychiatric nurse, so unsophisticated that she thought herself immune to childhood influences," they would say. What a joke! I knew I was projecting my fears into the situation but I was doing so on the basis of experience. Our hospital staff laughed at the behavior of patients every day, and I had no reason to believe the counseling center would be any different. Dramatically picturing the scene in my mind's eye, I sobbed all the way home, scarcely avoiding traffic mishaps.

The presentation I made during that session was unlike my demeanor in any other realm of my life. As a nurse, I was skilled, knowledgeable, and confident. I had been promoted to charge nurse within six months of finishing nursing school. I had won the respect of the physicians with whom I worked and had received praise from my hospital supervisor for my natural leadership abilities.

As a student, I was serious, focused, and felt myself to be an appreciated presence in the classroom by most of my instructors. As a wife, I was loving, loyal, thoughtful, and ever available to support my husband.

As a therapy client, I was apparently hyperemotional, confused, and ashamed, for reasons that remained outside my awareness.

Following our first appointment, I immediately felt emotionally compromised and didn't want to go back. I'd blown the "professional issues" plan with my display of sorrow. Yet I knew that my application for graduate school would be weak without this year of therapy. To make matters worse, the sorrow hadn't stopped at the door when I left his office. It not only persisted but, almost immediately, seemed to develop a life of its own. I began to experience unexpected periods of weeping that became problematic due to their unpredictability.

I felt I had naively painted myself into a corner. I could not reasonably abort my plans for therapy and, for reasons beyond my comprehension, the idea of continuing seemed excruciatingly unbearable to me. I decided I would regroup myself, stay in therapy a few months— just long enough to be able to claim I had done it—then I would terminate with no hard feelings and no damage done. As for my effusive sorrow, it would eventually subside, or so I hoped.

Since I now doubted my ability to contain emotional expressions that might win a negative judgment from Chuck, I appealed to what I hoped was his own sense of justice concerning the process of diagnosing patients. In the next several sessions, I reiterated my objections to the diagnostic process, hoping he would get the not too cryptic message that I didn't feel safe from professional name-calling. I reasoned that if I couldn't keep myself from appearing "crazy," I could perhaps influence Chuck not to say much about it to others.

Another difficulty I encountered in establishing a reasonable comfort level in therapy was the use of a tape recorder. As an intern, Chuck was required to tape our sessions for his supervisor to review for comment. After a few sessions, I began to feel that Chuck would honor my requests for no labels and absolute confidentiality. However, I had no influence over this nameless, faceless supervisor. What if he or she hobnobbed with the clinical faculty and somehow it was communicated that a crazy woman was applying for graduate school? What if the faculty member was able to put the pieces together and identify me? I was paranoid of any "leaks" as to my identity. At that time, I reasoned my paranoia was related to my graduate school application. I didn't know then that twelve years would pass before my awareness would open to the deeper reasons for my fear of exposure.

I asked Chuck to check to see if there was any way to dispense with the tape recorder. He returned the following week reporting that there wasn't, but offered instead, "Would you like to meet my supervisor?" I didn't even have to think about it. Unequivocally, "No" was my reply. All I needed was for this person to know me by my appearance. That would really preserve my anonymity! I knew my fear of exposure was excessive and didn't really make sense in the present context. This recognition, however, only enhanced my growing concern that I was really crazy and that, through therapy, the whole world would know soon!

Despite what seemed like a plethora of irrational fears, I was slowly bonding to Chuck as our weekly meetings grew in number. He was kind, attentive, and accepting. More behaviors that made no sense to me began to surface, and I was given to the procedure of reporting my self-observations to Chuck, always attaching the statement, "I don't know why." I would experience unexpected sensations of panic with no identifiable triggers, responding with "I don't know why." I felt an increasing urgency to self-destruct, again stating, "I don't know why."

Finally, Chuck asked, "What difference would it make if you knew why?" The question shook me deeply. Was he annoyed by my self-questioning? Would he abandon me if I persisted? To know the why of my behavior seemed like my only ticket to sanity. If I could connect my behavior to the purpose it was serving, I wouldn't feel so crazy. I couldn't find the words to express this thought, so I resolved not to query "why" anymore.

A few months into our relationship, Chuck initiated our session with, "Leia, I've been thinking about your work with me, and I feel you might really benefit by working with someone with more experience than what I have. You seem to be a very complex person, and I would like for you to get maximum benefit from your time spent in therapy." He heaved a great sigh, as though he had dreaded breaking the news.

My internal reactions were several and conflicting. Part of me rejoiced. Here was my ticket out of therapy! An opening had been created, and I could slip through the crack between Chuck and the next therapist. Also, a part of me was flattered. He had described me as "complex" and that could be taken as a compliment. However, the deepest part of me felt sad and ashamed. He must feel burdened by me, I thought. Processing my feelings like a small child, I told myself, I must remember not to ask for too much, and be more moderate and considerate in emotional expressions. He will abandon me if I don't do it right. I wasn't aware of how regressed and immature my thoughts and feelings seemed to be. I had risked more than I had planned in the beginning, and it was turning out to be a mistake. Tears burned in my eyes as I said, "I'd really rather not change therapists at this point." I felt like a child begging. To myself I thought, He must think I am crazy and doesn't want to work with me; complex is a euphemism for crazy.

"I was afraid you might feel you were being rejected," he said. "That's not my intent, and if you're willing to work with me knowing my feeling of limitation, I'm willing to hang in there. I just want you to know that people with more experience are available to you." I made a mental note to try to be "better" and hoped this wouldn't come up again.

But, as it turned out, I couldn't be "better." In fact, I was getting worse. Panic attacks were more frequent and severe. Outbursts of unexplainable grief were a real problem. My ability to control my emotions was weakening. I often wept copiously in the car on my way to and from work or school for no identifiable reason. At one point, I began weeping in the middle of a very impersonal, scientific social psychology class. I tried to invent plausible explanations for my emotions. Chuck was becoming increasingly important to me because he was the only one with whom I shared these feelings, but even with him I was careful to minimize my descriptions of their intensity.

The winter holidays came and there was a break in our therapy. Then, in January, Chuck was hospitalized for an appendectomy. I was aware that I was gradually developing a preoccupation with suicidal fantasies, and I was considering sharing them with Chuck when he recovered from his surgery. I often struggled, when driving on the freeway, with the impulse to turn at high speed into the concrete abutment dividing the lanes. I also had a dim awareness that I sometimes had participated in dangerous sports such as parachuting, secretly hoping I would die in an accident. It would be a huge leap in trust to tell Chuck, but my thoughts of suicide were growing increasingly comfortable to me and I was becoming worried about myself.

Before broaching the subject of suicide with Chuck, I settled on a different, less threatening tact for disclosure. Without first discussing it, I brought a photograph album to our first meeting following the winter break. I studied Chuck's face very carefully as he turned the pages examining the black and white photographic testimonials to my life as a child. I know now that I was testing him. I wanted him to notice that I didn't smile for a single photograph until I reached young womanhood. I wanted him to comment on how strange that was. Even more, I wanted him to see the wide-eyed look of fear in my eyes as a child. I thought I saw the fear but I couldn't understand what it meant, and I didn't trust my own judgment. If Chuck saw it too, then I would know it was real and my perception would be validated. I hoped Chuck might magically help me find the meaning of it. He commented that I bore a stronger resemblance to my mother than my father, and he thanked me somewhat awkwardly for bringing the album. He didn't seem clear about my expectations of him, and I felt embarrassed for having wanted something I couldn't articulate. He seemed aware that I was wanting something, but he didn't appear to know what it was and I couldn't, at that point, explain it to him. I was simply too confused. I left feeling mildly unfulfilled. I wasn't sure what he had seen in those pictures. I gave him the benefit of the doubt, hoping he had perceived my desperation and would formulate a plan to manage it.

The suicidal fantasies were, by now, quite elaborate. The more I revealed in therapy, the more suicidal I felt. My sharing the photograph album had intensified my self-destructive preoccupation. The vision I repeatedly played in my head was that I would obtain a single-edge razor blade and, on a cool, sunny day, I would walk down to the creek behind my house, dissect my left forearm at the wrist, find the radial artery, and slice it open. I imagined how it would feel as my strength and pain flowed out onto the ground with each heartbeat. I visually imagined the vivid red of my blood, with rhythmic spurts as it fell to the ground. I further imagined gradually losing consciousness of my surroundings and passing into infinite peace. These images became quite hypnotic, and I often had to shake myself loose from the peace they seemed to promise.

I knew that if I shared this with Chuck he might diagnose me with Borderline Personality Disorder but, in light of the present circumstances, labels receded in importance. At times, I really felt as though my life was hanging by a thread, so I took the chance. I told Chuck I was entertaining thoughts of suicide.

"What do you imagine would happen after your death?" he asked.

"I don't know," I answered. And, I really don't care, I thought.

"Most people who commit suicide have a plan for punishing someone living, or they imagine a better afterlife," he continued. I froze, trying to be sure I understood what he was saying. Was he giving me the latest research findings on the antecedent conditions of suicide? Did I understand his response correctly, I wondered, never sure of my perceptions. I had just bared my soul to him and there he sat, seemingly indifferent, perhaps slightly curious, but entirely missing the significance of my revelation and its implications for me and for us.

"What would your epitaph read?" he asked lightly. I was confused. Was he trying to exercise a paradoxical maneuver to provoke my anger to replace my depression? Did he care about my survival? To some extent, his detachment was working. The therapist part of me wanted to lean forward, grab him by the shirt collar, shake him, and scream, "Can't you see there's a child dying in here?" The words would have made no sense and I didn't have the emotional strength to speak them. I felt I was a fool; I must have interpreted Chuck's kindness toward me as meaning more than it did. I wanted him to care. I wanted my life to matter to someone. I felt utterly alone and abandoned, with nowhere to find a safe haven from the mysterious lure of death.

"Nothing," I said, "I don't think my epitaph would say anything. I can't think of a thing." My voice dropped to a whisper as my energy collapsed under the weight of the recognition that I was not going to be taken seriously.

This moment was the turning point in our work together. What I had hoped he would say was something like, "I can hear how desperate you are feeling. How can I help you create safety for yourself so that we can look deeper into the sources of your pain?" Instead, I interpreted his reaction to me as saying, "I don't believe you and I refuse to take you seriously."

He did have good reasons for assuming I wouldn't act on my suicidal impulses. Much of each weepy session was taken up with my rumination about admission to graduate school, complete with plans and fantasies about the future. The greater part of my consciousness was clearly invested in life. Only a small aspect of me had reached this critical point, beyond which I could not advance without support and protection, something Chuck was not able or willing to give.

The existential choices left open for me were several. I could persevere on the present course and risk self-destruction, punishing Chuck and myself to prove a point. This very thought seemed silly and held the potential to accomplish nothing. I could continue to beg for full recognition of my unexplainable pain, at the expense of my already compromised self-worth. I doubted our chances for success, and time was running out on Chuck's internship. Or, I could seal closed this present experience and figure myself lucky for having gotten as far as I did. The third option seemed most reasonable, and I proceeded to take ambivalent steps toward ending my relationship with Chuck.

Termination was more easily said than done. Despite my disappointment in the outcome of treatment, I really liked Chuck. He was kind, fun, and reasonable. He filled a void in my life and termination would create a vacancy. I still felt raw and unprotected following my suicide debates. I concluded that a little comfort would be better than no comfort at all.

I tried to terminate twice before Chuck's year of internship ended. He and I colluded, however, in keeping termination from happening until the very last minute. I felt appreciated by him and welcomed his talking me out of terminating. At times I even remember feeling special, and those tender feelings still bring tears to my eyes.

It was difficult for me to let go of Chuck. He had represented a hope for salvation from my as yet undisclosed injury. I had no way of knowing whether the opportunity for inner healing would present itself again. I regretted the time pressure we'd both been aware of throughout the year and, most of all, I was sad to see him go.

A few months after Chuck's departure, I was accepted into graduate school. I was gratified that the year I'd spent in anguish had paid off, although I had strong reservations about continuing with a new therapist. Two years later, my first child was born and the cycle of life went on, and on, and on.

Chuck:

Leia first came to the Georgia State University Counseling Center in October 1976. A senior counselor interviewed her and assigned her to me—a green-as-grass psychology intern. Leia's presenting problem was job dissatisfaction. She was working at the time as a charge nurse in a hospital psychiatric unit. On a fifty-item problem checklist, she marked three items as most problematic: doubting wisdom of my vocational choice, feelings too easily hurt, and worrying about unimportant things. The counselor who interviewed Leia may have regarded her as a fairly typical client and, therefore, appropriate for an intern to work with. He also noted that she "should be short-term."

Well, appearances were deceiving, as they often are with survivors of sexual abuse. Leia's account of those early sessions reveals that her inner experience was a roiling cascade of anxiety and self-doubt. What I saw was a bright, articulate, and intense young woman. I was not aware of the storm beneath the surface. Even when the storm broke, and Leia began to weep in that first session, I still did not fathom how difficult the whole process was for her.

It is easy to lose sight of how vulnerable therapy clients can feel when revealing who they are. As difficult as it is for clients in general to do this, it must be excruciating for survivors. They believe with an intense conviction that secrecy protects and openness endangers.

Of course, I had no idea that sexual abuse was the issue here. It was 1976 and the conventional wisdom was that incest was a rare occurrence. Nowadays it is one of the first things I would consider; then it would have been one of the last. In fact, I do not believe I ever thought of childhood sexual abuse as the source of Leia's distress.

The phrase "I'll believe it when I see it" can be turned on its head to read "I'll see it when I believe it." What I believed in those days was the theory of Transactional Analysis, and that is what I "saw" when

I worked with Leia. We discussed the "Critical Parent messages" she received as a child (for example, "Don't Feel What You Feel"), and how such messages were toxic elements in her life-script. Theory is, however, a slender reed to cling to in a choppy sea, and Leia was having a hard time staying afloat.

I must have been somewhat aware of this to have offered her the opportunity to work with a more experienced therapist but, once again, I believe I did not fully grasp the depth of her distress.

One thing that misled me was how well Leia could seem to function. She was something of a dynamo, working full time and going to school. I have since seen this trait in other survivors: a remarkable capacity for hard work, almost as if their worth depended upon it, as perhaps it does.

It is difficult to recollect details after a span of fifteen years, but I do recall a few. The time Leia brought in her family photo album, I can remember feeling anxious—was I aware of her intense scrutiny?—and going blank. Afterward, it seemed like a lost opportunity. It was.

On another occasion I told Leia that the Critical Parent messages she was struggling with were like spells or curses, but the room in which we met was curse-proof and she was safe there. It was an idea she seemed to like, because she often referred to "our curse-proof room."

The real work of breaking the curse, however, was not to begin until years later. The rest of this book tells the story of that work.

3
CHAPTER

*C*huck's leaving created the vacancy I had imagined and feared it would. My experience with him had been satisfying enough that I was willing to override my apprehension and try again. I entered therapy once more at the Counseling Center with a woman Chuck had recommended. However, we were not a good match for reasons I can't explain, even now. Whatever the essential ingredient is that is necessary for therapy to thrive, it was not present, and all the good will and best intentions in the world couldn't create it. We ended our relationship after an unproductive year.

Although that relationship had foundered, I persisted in my search to find someone with whom I could comfortably interact. Meanwhile my first son had been born, so I was facing a whole new set of issues when I entered therapy with a man recommended by my faculty advisor. This match was not merely unproductive; it was outright harmful. I spent an entire year trying to be a good client in order to avoid my therapist's criticism, professionally labeled as "confrontation." This therapist prided himself on making clients accept responsibility for their life predicaments and feelings. For me it meant facing weekly sessions of personal condemnation. I gradually developed a perception of therapy as sadomasochistic interaction. Ending the relationship was the only healthy choice I could make.

Comparing my second and third therapy experiences to my encounter with Chuck, I concluded I must have been spoiled. I'd experienced something almost magical with Chuck that I wasn't able to recreate with other therapists. I also assumed the reason for this was that something was wrong with me that made me unfit even for therapy. Not only was I struggling through life, I was even a failure at therapy.

I had nearly resolved to discontinue treatment permanently. It was not that I felt "cured" or even "improved," but I felt discouraged and hopeless that anyone could help me progress beyond where I was. My self-esteem was seriously damaged from my previous therapy experiences, and I blamed myself for the failures. When I finally resumed treatment, it was only because I was under pressure from graduate school faculty to do so. My life had become overly full and frantic by the time I entered therapy with Dr. Morgan Worthy at the Georgia State University Counseling Center. I was doing so under duress because of a faculty member who had supervised some of my clinical work. I was not an enthusiastic client.

My life circumstances by this time included parenting a very temperamental toddler, working as a nurse to support my education, carrying a full academic load in my fourth year of graduate training, and losing my husband's emotional companionship to alcohol. My toddler was a poor sleeper, making me a poor sleeper. The stress in my life was acute and visible to the most casual observer. The era was mid-feminism, and women were struggling to "have it all." I was having way too much. Feminism in those days meant the masculinization of women through the rejection of traditional female roles. I had the impression that my caring for our son was judged by certain faculty members as my failing at feminism. The faculty member who had commented on my chronic appearance of distress was not kind in her demand that I enter therapy. She was a single woman with a career in academia and she had little tolerance for a baby-toting student.

"Why don't you leave him in day care? There's no empirical evidence to suggest it is harmful," she'd said with thinly masked contempt in her voice.

I knew any attempt to explain my circumstances would be futile. I didn't want to risk my career in an argument with her. She would never understand that day care centers don't keep sick children and my son had chronically infected ears. Nor did I feel safe in disclosing the unavailability of my spouse resulting from his addiction. I had learned that the less time my son spent in the company of other sniffing, coughing youngsters the healthier he was, so I took him with me whenever I could, despite the raising of eyebrows by certain faculty members. I didn't feel I had a safe choice. More than once, professors questioned means to my priorities. The message to me seemed to be that a serious student would not procreate during academic training! I knew only a small minority of students started families in graduate school. I had broken an unwritten policy and I felt I was being punished for it. My feelings of self-worth seemed, during this period, to be continuously on the line. No matter what I did, I seemed to encounter somebody's disapproval. I was emotionally exhausted by the effort required to keep my family and career going. My personal needs often sank to the lowest position on the list of priorities.

Not only did I feel persecuted over family loyalties, but also I felt personally violated by various graduate school training experiences. Supervision was frequently targeted at the character traits of student therapists rather than the quality of work conducted. Supervision most often occurred in groups where one's personal vulnerabilities could be splayed open before one's peers. The process of supervision contained so much risk for me, as vulnerable as I felt, that very little actual learning occurred, since all my energy was spent surviving the ordeals associated with the process.

One day, the same faculty member who insisted I re-enter therapy to sever the bond joining me to my tiny child demonstrated no self-restraint in pointing out to our supervision group that the way I sat in a chair was like that of women who had been raped. Naturally, the other four students in my group all turned to stare at me as my face flushed and my jaw locked to hold back my rage over the unprovoked attack. My mind filled with bitter hatred for people in general who misuse their scholarly authority to justify acts of unnecessary cruelty, and for this woman in particular. My heart raced as I fought back tears. I promised myself I would never mistreat another human the way I was being mistreated. I was learning the importance of kindness through experiences of psychological sadism.

When I made an appointment with Dr. Worthy, I was angry. I was angry about feeling forced into therapy by a faculty member whose own problems dwarfed mine by comparison. I was angry about the lack of connection I'd felt in the two previous years of my therapy, which accomplished nothing but the squandering of greatly needed money. I was angry about my husband's lack of involvement or help with raising our son. And I was angry that no one seemed to recognize or care that the burdens I lived under were excessive. For me, therapy represented one more demand—an hour a week I didn't have to spare— to listen to someone tell me I was an inadequate human being. My expectations of therapy were grim. It is difficult for me to comprehend today why I continued my training as a psychologist, when I had so little confidence in the profession. I clung tenaciously to the belief that I would be different.

Morgan Worthy was like a zephyr in a room of stale air. He was soft and approachable in appearance, with graying hair and beard, and rounded facial features. He was soft-spoken and non-aggressive from our very first meeting. He assumed a posture of being curious about me without implying the need for me to change, either for his entertainment or his own sense of self-worth. I couldn't resist liking him from the moment of our first meeting, despite my vast reservoir of anger.

Morgan was interested in dreams and urged me to record and bring to therapy any dreams that occurred between sessions. I have always been an active dreamer, and it sounded like it might be fun to explore the meaning of my dream images. I began to toy with the notion that therapy might not be so punitive after all.

I wanted to turn loose of my anger because I sensed I could gain something of value from this man, and anger could prevent me from doing so. I brought up the issue of anger early in our work together, trying to get enough resolution to allow me to proceed more comfortably in therapy.

"I know how resentful I feel about things that have happened in previous therapy situations, and I know I need to let go of it, but I don't quite know how. I guess I need some kind of reassurance from you that if my anger oozes out around the edges that you won't leave me." I'd said it with some trepidation. I certainly didn't want to slaughter a relationship that seemed rich in potential.

Morgan sat quietly for a moment, then softly replied, "Leia, I think I'm pretty good at letting people have their feelings, but I need to qualify that. If you were to make me the target of your anger, and it were to start to feel hurtful to me, I'd have to stop. I'm only human." He had set a limit, and modeled self-protection in one sentence. I admired him for that, and hoped I could keep the reins pulled in on my accumulation of resentment.

"How about if I work hard to make sure you know my anger isn't focused at you?" I bargained; "Unless, of course, something comes up between us that we need to work out."

And so we negotiated back and forth our various needs around anger in such a manner that I felt comfortably juxtaposed with him. Ironically, the issue never came up between us again. I needed the reassurance that I could be angry and, knowing there was a mechanism where I could, I never felt the need.

Anger and fear about my various life circumstances surfaced in my dreams, however. Morgan consistently responded by carefully qualifying his reactions to my dreams.

"I want you to know that what I'm offering you is my reaction to your dreams. These are not my dreams and I don't want to damage the integrity of your dreams. If I ever say anything that makes you feel like I'm doing that, I want you to stop me."

My trust in this man soared! He was making me the authority on myself. My dear God! What a novel idea!

Morgan's style was to invite rather than demand, and my dreams were open and rich that year. I had recurrent dreams about the occult, which I judged to be descriptive of my perception of graduate school experiences.

I am at a church across the street from my old high school. It is situated on a corner lot. I enter the church and am horrified that to my right is an altar upon which the bloody dead bodies of children are stacked. There is an evil priestess, dressed in a habit with a trident in her hand, standing just behind the pile of bodies. Another priestess is gliding back and forth between the pews, eyeing me and my son, Drake, who has appeared behind me. Somehow I know I can't leave without being killed, although the evil priestess really wants my son for sacrifice. I am terrified. Somehow my husband and two family friends manage to rescue me but for some reason can't get to Drake. As we are driving away, I am looking at the church through the rear window of the car. I am miserable with fear that I won't get back in time to save him. The anguish I feel is nearly unbearable, and I promise myself I will go back and save him as I begin to realize this is a dream and I can control the outcome.

Morgan read my dream with the same serious expression to which I had become accustomed in our interaction. He pointed out a similarity between my dream scenarios and my feelings about graduate school: that it appeared sacred from the outside but was dangerous to my son and me once inside. He commented on the proximity of the church to the high school, suggesting that the dream incorporated "higher education." He noted the attire of the priestesses and that they weren't what they appeared to be. And finally he commented on the tridents.

"Different theorists regard dream symbols differently," he said, "but there is one thing all the big dream theorists seem to agree on, and that is that the number three has something to do with sex."

We both started to laugh. My amusement was that psychology has a reputation for its preoccupations with sex, and to be so certain of the meaning of the number three seemed downright silly to me. I still find humor when absolute positions are taken with such an inexact science. I enjoyed Morgan's break from the somber, immensely.

Two things were accomplished by Morgan's sharing of his impressions. One was that for the first time in more than three years of therapy, a therapist had mentioned sex. Despite my studies of psychodynamic theory, which advocates that psychological disturbances are the result of faulty psychosexual development, it never occurred to me to wonder why my own therapists never asked about or mentioned sex. Retrospectively, I imagine I presented clear nonverbal cues that certain topics were to be avoided—with sex heading the list. The second was that for the second time, someone was suggesting sexual assault (the first being my professor mentioned earlier). The trident, if it indeed represented something sexual, had been used to impale and kill children. It was both frightening and interesting to me to consider that sex might somehow be associated with danger for me. But I easily dismissed the thought by reasoning that dream interpretation has little respectability in modern psychology. A trident could mean anything, I thought to myself. It was a weapon in my dream, an instrument of execution. I pictured a trident in the hand of Neptune, wielding power from his subterranean abode. I turned the dream over and over in my mind until I found an interpretation of the trident that didn't involve sex. The trident was a symbol of power in the hands of gods, or in this case, priestesses. I agreed the priestesses represented my faculty and the trident suggested the power they held to terminate my training. Sex definitely was not necessary to explain the trident. The undisclosed fact of my sexuality was that I was very conflicted about sex, but my self-concept was too fragile to allow disclosure to anyone of yet another flaw in my personhood. I kept myself much too busy to think about it.

Dreams are persistent and repetitive. My own dreams often leave me feeling humble, sometimes even foolish, as if to say, "Okay, dummy. Since you didn't catch on to that one, let me say it another way, and another way, and another way until you finally get it!"

As our work with dreams continued, so did the symbols of disturbance with sex reoccur, becoming gradually more dramatic.

I am a waitress in a little log cabin cafe in the West. It is sunset and I am at work, wearing a white skirt. All at once I realize I've menstruated and blood is showing through on the back of my skirt. For some reason, I cannot go and change my clothing; I have to continue to work wearing this skirt. I turn my body as I'm serving the customers, trying to prevent them from seeing the blood on my skirt.

I brought the dream to my therapy, with some feeling of embarrassment. Morgan was very respectful as he pointed out that my skirt was white, which is often a symbol of purity or innocence, that clothing often represents the "persona," or public appearance a person tries to maintain, and that in the dream I am in the process of serving food to the public, which is often a symbol of nurturing or caregiving. Finally, softly, almost cautiously, he offered, "It appears you may have concerns about being spotted. Maybe there is something you don't want those you nurture to know about you." My mind drew a blank although my breath came noticeably faster. The implication was that I was keeping a secret. I didn't have a clue as to what it might be. I was thoroughly confused and didn't know how to answer Morgan's quizzical look.

My dreams seemed to become annoyed by my persistent ignorance and at last provided a dramatization so perverse that it became a new secret for me to keep.

I am in an upstairs room where the ceilings slant with the roofline. I am a little girl and I'm naked. There is another little girl and I am to perform cunnilingus on her. I don't understand why. When I do so, a vomitus-like substance mixed with bits of fabric is expelled from her vagina into my mouth. The taste and texture are putrid and completely repulsive. I am gagged by a bolus of this substance in my throat. My grandmother is watching, disapprovingly, and I wake up, struggling to breathe.

Upon waking from this dream, I was physically shaking, and I judged this dream was too perverse to share, even with Morgan. I wanted him to continue to hold some respect for me, and I couldn't imagine what he might think of someone who could produce such a sexually disturbed story. I felt humiliated and shamed. How could I have produced such a sick dream?

The earlier dream about being spotted had become a prophecy. I now had a conscious secret to hide, and it affected my relationship with Morgan in ways I could not explain. The dream had been so upsetting to me that it stayed on my mind for days. I could remember the texture and taste of the putrid bolus with no sense of what it meant and no courage to discuss it with anyone.

My time with Morgan was coming to an end. It was nearly time for me to begin my psychology internship away from the university. I have no way of knowing now whether I'd have ever found the nerve to discuss the dream even if I'd not been restricted by time. I do know there was nothing Morgan could have done to make it any more comfortable or safe for me to tell.

The paradox for me as a client was that I couldn't bring myself to share the dream without knowing what it meant, and I couldn't know the meaning without sharing it. I was so caught up in my own disgust that I couldn't think rationally about its meaning. I was not even remotely willing to consider the possibility that I had been sexually violated as a child. In the absence of any memory or anchor to justify producing such an atrocity, I rationalized that Morgan wouldn't be able to tell me anything more than what I already knew. Worse yet, he might concur with my obnoxious professor and suggest something about a sexual assault or childhood sexual experience.

There was a part of me that wanted desperately to tell the dream, but the greater part thought it best not to. My conflict stayed in the forefront of my mind, making the last few months of my work with Morgan mildly uncomfortable. I was afraid to say very much about even the most unrelated topics, fearing that some reference to the dream would slip out. I became superficial and cowardice undermined my self-respect. My dreams became both sparse and shallow. My discipline to record them was sporadic. I had gone as far as I could go without taking what seemed like a terrifying risk, and I wasn't willing to take such a risk.

Finally it was time for me to begin my internship and, with a mixture of relief and regret, I stopped seeing Morgan. I was filled with appreciation for his kind support of me during my last year on campus. He had re-established my trust in the beneficial possibilities of therapy, and he sent me on my way with his blessing. The effects of the dream were eventually suppressed by me as I went on with my life.

4
CHAPTER

*F*ive years had passed since my year of therapy with Morgan. I had completed graduate school, given birth to my second son, was employed part time developing psychological support services for an acute care hospital, and had opened my private practice when I decided to see Dr. Edward W.L. Smith for supervision only. Personal therapy was a thing of the past. Nobody could force or coerce me into therapy against my will. I was a free agent, and I felt relieved in knowing therapy was a free choice, not a mandate. My negative therapy experiences lingered in the back of my mind, and I held a clear position that I wouldn't put myself through the pain again.

I had never met Edward, although I knew he taught psychology as an adjunct professor at my alma mater. I was aware that he'd written a book entitled Sexual Aliveness, and that he was successful as a writer. His professional presentations and accomplishments were regularly listed in the faculty newsletter at Georgia State University where I was now a part-time instructor. I placed a call to him to see if he would be willing to supervise my clinical work, fully expecting an indignant secretary to return my call informing me that the esteemed Dr. Smith didn't see any but the most highly evolved individuals and, with my being an insignificant unknown, I didn't have the proper qualifications to become his supervisee. I was surprised, and not altogether relieved, when he personally returned my call, chatted in a cordial yet businesslike manner, and suggested we meet once to determine whether we felt we could work together. An appointment time was established and that was that.

I instantly developed a mild fear of entering a relationship with this man, but the appointment was set and I didn't want my pervasive cowardice to gain the upper hand. I realized my fantasy of being rejected was really my wish; had he rejected my inquiry, I'd have had a guilt-free reason to avoid another potentially dangerous situation.

My first meeting with Edward was both formal and congenial. I was surprised, upon meeting him, at his youth. I had expected a man in his fifties or early sixties. I was incorrect in my estimation by nearly fifteen years, and I was a little disappointed. An older man would have seemed safer. I was also impressed by the fact that such a young man had already accomplished so much professionally. I felt humble and honored that he agreed to meet with me, and my apprehension abated somewhat.

By way of appearance, Edward was of medium height with a small frame and hands. He had medium brown hair and a beard. His deep brown eyes had a way of smiling, which I found very engaging. We discussed the general characteristics of my caseload, and he described his general approach to case consultation and supervision which was, as he put it, "to work with the person of the therapist." He seemed pleasant, reasonable, knowledgeable, and genuine. He didn't seem to manifest the pomposity I feared he might, and he was not at all condescending. We decided we could work together and, because of my small caseload, set the frequency of our visits at once per month.

I exercised careful control during our year and a half of supervision to make certain it didn't accidentally or spontaneously evolve into psychotherapy. I revealed very little of my personal life or past circumstances. In fact, given the context we had adopted, self-revelation about anything other than my responses to clients would have seemed out of place. Every now and then, though, something personal would slip through and I would watch his response as though to judge whether or not he approved. In retrospect, I can see that I was assessing his trustworthiness.

I also used another method to test Edward's trustworthiness and competence. I would describe situations brought to me by my clients and ask for his reaction. He always took a sincere approach to his discussion of cases. His gaze would uplift and he would occasionally stroke his beard, as though in deep thought before responding. Sometimes I would choose cases to discuss that were similar to my own life experiences. And I watched. He was kind, thoughtful, and reasonable, never belittling or making fun of pain felt by others. I liked and soon respected him, but still had no intentions of changing our relationship in any way. I felt lucky and appreciative to have him as a supervisor.

I had been seeing Edward for supervision for about eighteen months when he invited me to attend a one-day workshop he was conducting on embodied Gestalt practice. He suggested I might benefit more from our supervision if I had an understanding of the methods he used when working as a therapist. My immediate response to the invitation was to internally inventory all of the reasons I shouldn't go. The workshop was to be held on a Saturday and I hated to commit more time away from my children, knowing how they eagerly anticipated spending time with me. I internally argued that I would not have the energy to spend in a workshop on my day off. Yet I needed the continuing education credits to maintain my psychology license. I also felt a sense of obligation to Edward. His suggestion was reasonable, and I felt I would not be showing the proper respect and appreciation if I didn't go. I created an anticipation of safety for myself by reasoning that I could sit back in the workshop and observe without much strain, and I was sure it would be interesting. After considerable deliberation, overcoming great internal resistance, I decided to go.

Heartwood was the name given the log house where the workshop was held, an hour's drive from the city. The setting was rural and heavily wooded. The October day was cool and overcast. About twelve people arrived for the training; nearly all were therapists.

Embodied Gestalt practice is quite different from what most people imagine when hearing the word "therapy." Most therapies rely on talking, thinking, and working through life's problems to achieve understanding or "insight," which will then lead to behavior change. Embodied Gestalt practice focuses more on expression than understanding. The underlying assumption is that throughout our lives we have experiences with our environment and other people in the course of satisfying our needs. As needs arise and are met, different needs arise and so on. The difficulty comes when needs arise and actions taken by the person to meet the needs directly are blocked or fail to lead to satisfaction. For example, a hungry child may forage for food in the kitchen before dinner and receive punishment from an angry parent. The child's efforts to self-soothe hunger have been blocked, and it is assumed the memory of the punishment or blocked expression is held on a body level. The child may feel very angry with the parent but would not dare express that anger for fear of further punishment, blocking another move to action and so on. As the person travels through life, he or she resorts to various strategies for inhibiting action or manipulating others in order to satisfy needs. These strategies for meeting needs become "embodied," and the assumption is that if the person can express the blocked impulses to action, behavioral change will result, yielding healthier self-supportive interaction with the environment.

The difference between this form of treatment and traditional talk therapies is evident from the beginning. The therapist doesn't require a thorough knowledge of the client's history, but works instead with bodily manifestations in the immediate situation, such as sensations of heat, cold, tingling, pain, or tension. The therapist can also use appearances of the body to determine an appropriate treatment intervention.

The workshop began with Edward saying a few words about his personal philosophy of embodied Gestalt practice, after which he led an exercise for participants to explore and focus on physical sensations and areas of tension. Once the exercise was completed, each member shared with the group his or her "discovery" of bodily awareness, followed by Edward inviting volunteers interested in working individually with him to the center of the group.

During the morning session, Edward facilitated physical expression of two individual participants, one after the other, in a way that seemed nearly magical to me. With very little information on either person, he artfully honed in on the metaphor for the person's life and invented a method for expressing blocked energy that seemed perfectly matched to the individual in that moment—I was impressed!

We took a lunch break, and I strolled over the grounds feeling my anxiety starting to mount; I wanted to be the next volunteer. I felt almost enough courage to ask but feared that he would refuse, telling me he had something else planned for the afternoon, or someone else had already made a request for his time, or that he would offer some other polite, valid reason for rejecting my initiative. Mustering my courage and also anticipating rejection, arguing with the voice of reason in my head, I approached Edward and, to my surprise, pleasure, and horror, he agreed to work with me. His facial expression suggested a hint of his own surprise at my request.

The group reconvened in a large circle with some people sitting on floor cushions and others in chairs. I sat beside Edward on the floor and, to my dismay and embarrassment, I heard myself announce to him and the group that I was aware of having diminished sensation below my waist, as well as unexplained idiosyncratic pain in response to touch in both of my ankles. I immediately met with internal rebuke. How could you say such a thing in front of twelve strangers? a part of me demanded. I'll never see them again, I countered, and it won't matter.

Edward seemed unruffled by my disclosure and remained calm and attentive. He didn't seem to register the shock I was feeling. He asked if I would be willing to move to the center of the room and lie down on the bare mattress that had been used in the previous therapy demonstrations. I agreed, struggling to suppress rapidly mounting terror. He then asked my permission to place his hands in such a manner that my heart would be between them, one over my upper chest and the other on my upper back. It sounded a bit strange but I was willing. We positioned ourselves with me lying on my back facing the ceiling and him lying on his side to my right, holding my heart between his hands.

Nobody spoke for a time and I felt mildly conspicuous. Was I expected to do something? What was supposed to happen? I'd never read or heard of anything about this technique before, so I had no frame of reference for classification.

While I was lying there pondering whether or not to do anything, the reaction to this body intervention struck. Unexpectedly, without any verbal, visual, or auditory triggers, a great outpouring of grief rocked through my body. I lost contact with the linear awareness of time and I began to sob. At first I had no image whatsoever to which

I could connect my pain. Tears poured down the sides of my face, soaking my hair. The sounds rising from my throat were the whimpers of a small child.

Although I was aware of being the central figure in a room full of people, that fact seemed distant and insignificant. Edward spoke in near whispers, words of reassurance and support. I didn't feel compelled to disrupt the flow of emotions coursing through me, and I settled into the experience without fighting it. Gradually, an impression developed into an image in my mind's eye. I was upstairs in a house with a slanted ceiling that followed the roofline. There was a window in the end wall and I could see daylight streaming in. I was alone in this room and quite frightened, as though I expected something horrible to happen to me. I seemed to be crouched down beside a bed, hiding, not knowing from whom. I was aware that I was very young, and that I was wearing a dress. I was also wearing tiny black patent leather shoes that I remembered having as a small child.

My tears continued to flow. Edward softly asked, "How old are you?" I was mildly disoriented. I answered, "Maybe three." I told Edward about the room and my fear.

Finally, I heard a sob from the corner of the workshop room where a young anorexic woman had been seated earlier, and I gradually began to reconnect with my present environment. I was emotionally touched by the young woman's tears. In a way I could not explain, I felt validated by our shared emotion. Nearly an hour had passed since my work with Edward began. I was ready to stop for now. I sat up and, looking around the room through swollen eyes at the tender faces of others, I apologized for taking so much time and was reassured it hadn't been too long.

I returned to my place in the circle. Edward sat beside me and asked whether I would be comfortable with his discussing our work with the group. I gave my permission and sat listening, in a fog.

"Why did you work with her heart rather than her legs when she was complaining of problems in the lower portion of her body?" a person asked. Edward answered, "Reich talked about the legs being an extension of the pelvis. If there was trauma to the pelvis, I didn't want to retraumatize."

"You've discussed soft and hard body techniques in your writings. This was obviously a soft technique. Why did you choose this over other techniques?" another asked.

"If you'll look at Leia, she is soft in appearance. She is not a heavily muscled person; even her voice is soft. I chose a technique to match her body type. Had I used a hard technique, she would have experienced it as invasive . . . possibly traumatizing."

Another asked, "Are you concerned about her dissociating or becoming depersonalized?"

"No, I've known Leia for quite some time. I know her to be a very solid and well-grounded person psychologically."

I was relieved and reassured by the answer he gave to the last question. Still in a fog, I couldn't predict my state of being into the next moment. Edward sounded so sure of my mental stability that I was happy to accept his assessment as being true.

The workshop ended soon after my work with Edward. The group gradually broke up as evening approached. The drive home afterward was like a dream. I didn't know what the events of the day meant and my brain was too muddled to sort it out. I was too exhausted from my emotional experience to even listen to the radio. I was drained from the release of my emotions, and I felt a certain peacefulness. I was also mildly embarrassed about having been the center of attention for so long, but I was able to dismiss the feeling by telling myself I wouldn't see these people again.

Arriving home, I prepared dinner, as usual, played with the kids, as usual, and went through my normal routine as though nothing unusual had happened.

Edward:

Leia began with me with such ambivalence. The choice of supervisor, as the choice of a therapist, is often a highly complex matter, "overdetermined" by a variety of motives, some of which may be thoroughly outside of awareness. These so-called unconscious motives are often most interesting, as they are inferred or at least raised as possibilities in light of the information that later emerges. What could have been the factors that led Leia to choose me as a supervisor? On a conscious level, I was well qualified, had a lot of credentials, and was well reputed in the professional community. So were many others. But Leia knew I had recently published a book entitled Sexual Aliveness. She mentioned this in one of our early meetings, as I recall. At the time, that was the least known of my books, and yet it made an impression. Could it be that Leia was unconsciously anticipating that her supervisory relationship with me would evolve into a therapeutic one? Leia learned early on that my style of case consultation is "to work with the person of the therapist," focusing on who the therapist is, and how her or his being influences therapy, rather than focusing on the client as if a "case" independent of the therapist-client interaction. Yet, Leia chose to work with me. And, further, could it be that Leia was unconsciously anticipating that the content of our eventual, if not inevitable, therapeutic work would involve something having to do with sex? Perhaps to these ends, Leia tested me over and over, probably many more times than I ever knew. When I recognized a test, I can remember reminding myself of impeccability—breathe deeply and slowly, center yourself, listen well, be patient, hear her out, respond honestly without defense. She tested me and I passed the test. At later times Leia occasionally would test me again as if for reassurance of her decision to trust me. I knew the importance of her testing could not be overestimated.

Both Leia's hypervigilance and her obvious guardedness with me bespoke a decided self-protectiveness. One simple example I remember is her frequently announcing to me when her time was up, when actually we would have five or ten minutes remaining. She would seem eager to leave and do so with a certain celerity. I intuited that it was best to give her the option without challenge. I was quite sure there was a great deal going on with Leia below the surface, and I did not know what it was. My decision was to be patient.

My experience has taught me that in my daylong to weeklong workshops I offer something different from what I offer in my once-a-week or every-other-week fifty-minute hour format. The two formats complement one another. Since Leia had only read of my therapy work, I reasoned that she would be able to gain more from my case consultations if she could witness my working. So, as she has written, I encouraged her coming to Heartwood. On a more subtle level, I had a hunch that something good would come out of this, having something to do with her cautiousness with me. I just knew that the daylong intensive workshop has always proved for me to be a crucible in which transformations came about, almost always for the good.

I trusted, given Leia's high level of social and professional functioning, that she had the wherewithal to decline my invitation, either directly or indirectly through a socially acceptable excuse, if she were not ready for this experience. She obviously was ready, as we can see in hindsight. At Heartwood Leia requested to work. This is extremely important to keep in mind. The work can turn ill if it is undertaken with coercion. Ambivalence about working in such a workshop is common, but I always want to sense that the person is coming forward out of her or his own decision, that the urge to work exceeds the reluctance.

Having heard me give a cognitive introduction to my work and having had some demonstrations of it, Leia was an informed participant. She asked me to work with her and I agreed. The training model that I have used for years is an experiential one. I know that learning is most complete when gained through personal experience rather than secondhand accounts. So I was delighted at Leia's coming forward to learn by experiencing. I had no notion of what was to lie ahead of us.

I am so fascinated, still, by how a body phenomenon can convey so much meaning, by how, in Leia's case, her "diminished sensation below my waist, as well as unexplained idiosyncratic pain in response to touch in both of my ankles" told the story of her trauma. One way of saying this is that her body remembered. After checking me out carefully enough and bringing herself to the workshop setting where deep psychological work was being done, Leia was secure enough to allow her body to speak. It spoke in its own idiom of raw sensations. I translated these as follows: (1) "Diminished sensation" below the waist means a desensitization of the pelvis, which suggests a dulling of awareness around some issue involving the pelvis. I hypothesize a sexual trauma; (2) "Idiosyncratic pain in response to touch" in both ankles suggests a recalling of painful touch. I hypothesize that Leia has been grabbed or held by the ankles in connection with the hypothesized sexual trauma.

It was crucial that I not foist my hypotheses on Leia. My hypotheses were to alert me to possible issues as I watched and listened to Leia's presentation of herself. The important thing was for me to facilitate her process of self-exploration, for in this way her pride of self-discovery could, in part, offset the shock and pain of whatever she might discover. Besides, my hypotheses might not be accurate.

Sensing Leia's precarious balance between wanting to work and reluctance to work, I offered an invitation and proceeded, after her acceptance of my invitation, with care. I knew that to attempt any direct work with her pelvis would most likely be premature, eliciting considerable anxiety and possibly even recapitulating a feeling of violation if, indeed, Leia had a history of sexual trauma. The technique I chose was one that invites a gentle age regression and softening of any protective armoring around one's heart. As Leia lay there on her back, with her clear and explicit permission, I placed my hands on her chest and back with her heart between them. After a few quiet minutes, Leia relaxed her armoring and allowed her heart to "break." She sobbed as a small child. I supported Leia with touch and with soft supporting words.

Evolving out of her emotional expression came Leia's vivid visual image. She lifted her repression and remembered the scene which, in time, she would come to accept as the scene of her sexual trauma. I felt appreciative of Leia's courage and of the therapeutic power of properly applied body technique.

As I understand the process, what was required in this session were both my genuine humanness and the skillful application of a body technique. Neither, in itself, would have adequately supported Leia's self-exploration, emotional expression, and discovery. It was in the context of the "safe emergency" of the workshop that Leia was able to do this.

Traditionally, the model often used in psychotherapy is as follows:

Talking ☐ Memory ☐ Emotion

The talking between therapist and client leads to remembering the repressed experience, and it is this memory which, in turn, invites the associated emotion. Leia's work, however, demonstrates a less traditional model. In this case, the bodywork elicited the emotion directly, and from the expression of emotion, the associated memory was invited.

The latter model, then, is as follows:

Body Experience ☐ Emotion ☐ Memory

Leia still had a lot of work to do. She had experienced a crucial breakthrough, and now she needed to add some details to the memory, come to believe it, and to heal from it.

5
CHAPTER

The days and weeks following the workshop were filled with confusion and inner chaos as my psyche scrambled to reconstruct something to hold on to. My training as a psychologist became an instrument of torture with which I could beat myself, rather than the source of comfort it could have been. Not only was I in a great deal of pain and distress, but also I was evaluating my own symptoms and diagnosing myself from a professional perspective.

The day after the workshop, I woke up nearly incapacitated. Even the smallest task seemed to require enormous effort. I struggled through my ordinary activities in what seemed like slow motion. The very passage of time was distorted. My thinking was clouded, unfocused, and confused. Familiar food recipes now required careful study and concentration to produce. The amount of time required to complete a given task doubled or tripled. I was ineffective and inefficient at the simplest of tasks, such as loading the dishwasher. I viewed minor chores as insurmountable, and I desperately struggled to appear normal. And I was numb! I had no tears and no real thoughts about what had happened. I couldn't seem to think in the linear, logical fashion I'm so accustomed to, and my observation of my own behavior called into my mind old diagnostic labels like "retarded depression" and even "thought disorder," which is associated with psychotic conditions. I had brief fantasies of being hospitalized and losing everything I'd worked so hard for.

I told my family nothing, hoping they wouldn't notice my sudden impairment and start asking questions. I struggled alone to disguise my compromised functioning. What was there to tell? I had no idea of what yesterday's flashback was about and didn't know if I had invented something for my own entertainment, or if I was recalling something I had actually experienced. Even if it was a memory anchored to reality, I had no idea who I had been hiding from or why. Children become frightened by many things, some of which are harmless, and I had such a scant piece of information that I couldn't explain my present condition from my vision of being crouched by a bed. I cautioned myself not to make anything more out of it. Yet not to do so meant that my present symptoms had no cause, so I must be crazy. Reassurance was nowhere to be found.

Even without focusing on the flashback and what it meant, I could not ignore my present condition. This was Sunday and by Monday I would have to be a functional professional. I could not perform my professional duties in this psychological state. When evening fell without signs of improvement, I telephoned Edward to tell him what I was experiencing. I could barely formulate speech on the telephone. My mouth became dry and I couldn't bring to mind the words I wanted to speak. My voice sounded strange, monotonous, and distant to me. As obviously tormented as I was, I didn't want to need Edward and also, I didn't want to disappoint him since he had been so certain of my stability. I felt like I was painted into a corner. My behavior was not under my direct control, and I felt I had no choice but to ask for help.

Edward quietly listened over the telephone to my abbreviated description of my condition. I simply told him I was having trouble and he offered his first available appointment the following morning. He seemed to detect the urgency of the situation without my having to explain. I was grateful to have an appointment to focus on.

When I arrived at Edward's office Monday morning, my symptoms had not improved. My body felt rigid and I was still having difficulty speaking. I felt that I was actually positioned behind my body, that I was watching the world from somewhere behind my eyes. My voice sounded mechanical and distant to my own ears.

My strongest memory of our first therapy session together was the look of sadness on Edward's face. I had never before seen him look sad. I believed that his apparent sadness was not only in response to what was happening to me personally, but also for the trauma that befalls children everywhere. Sad for societies that tolerate and hide child abuse.

Sad for the twisted thinking in our own sexually disturbed culture that leads to the perverse directing of sexual energy toward children. Sad for the lasting effects of premature sexual interaction: shattered egos, frozen feelings, fear, and confusion. And sad for the legacy of sexual hurt and suffering that passes from generation to generation.

My observing ego, which was not much more than a watcher by this time, appreciated Edward's look of sadness. I could join with it, for sadness was the appropriate feeling response to a three-year-old child who had experienced a trauma severe enough to shatter her sense of self, haunting her, pruning her freedom for a full, healthy life expression thirty-five years after the fact.

My sense of an integrated whole self was indeed fractured. I was splitting into what Eric Berne described as "ego states," each based on some experience or interjected other person. In my journal, I identified each of six states:

Hurt Child
Tomboy/Protector
Child Discounting Mother
Unaware Father
Governing Ego
Edward

The strongest ego state present in our first session was the Tomboy and she bordered on being angry. She seemed to feel Edward was dangerous and also seemed in control of dissociation (the sense of oneself being outside of one's body). My Governing Ego was the observer, translator, and communicator. I could report what was going on internally, to some extent, but without emotional content or rational influence over other ego states. My voice relayed information to which I felt no personal connection. Edward seemed to take it as a good sign that he had a voice within my consciousness.

Conversation was a struggle that first session, yet two most important things were accomplished. The first was that, for the first time, I was entering therapy as a matter of clear distress. I had no auxiliary motives and I had a clear purpose, that of regaining my fragmented self. The second important moment came at the end when I stood up to leave.

Edward gave me an affectionate hug, which I tried to reciprocate despite my physical rigidity. Hugs had become our customary closing to sessions in the previous eighteen months. On this occasion he said to me, "No matter how badly you might feel, Leia, remember that whatever hurt you happened long ago. It isn't happening now."

We scheduled another appointment for me to cling to, and I tried to resume a normal life in the midst of emotional chaos. I was able to continue working as a psychologist, but was often dissociated, and learned that although I was sometimes unable to focus on what my clients were saying, I could almost miraculously muster an accurately empathetic response. My ego states were not working in coordination with one another, but they were cooperating to protect me from appearing crazy. I would watch an interaction between a client and me unfold in which I could scarcely make out the words of the client, much less grasp their meaning, and I would marvel at the eloquent response coming from me that seemed to make perfect sense to the client, judging from the facial appearance of relief. The entire exchange would be absolutely incomprehensible to me.

When I wasn't working, I was grieving and fighting with myself over whether anything ever really happened, fiercely arguing that I'd made something up to gain attention. While the evidence suggesting trauma was compelling, it was not concrete, and I sincerely didn't want to believe that anyone could have or would have sexually assaulted me at the age of three.

Edward and I had agreed to meet for weekly one-hour sessions. The spaces between sessions were filled with noisy internal dialogue and nightmares, often imbedded with clues. One day, after our first therapy appointment, I had this dream:

My mother-in-law and two nephews are on an outing together in a 1955 Chevrolet. They are somehow stopped and ambushed by a maniacal killer who slit their throats, killing all of them. I never see the killer. I omnisciently know of the event. They each bleed to death. In the dream I feel that bleeding to death isn't such a bad way to die. I am trying to find someone to bring the bodies back for proper burial. I am determined to do so.

The dream fit together neatly with the workshop flashback in some ways. It suggested a date for the trauma at 1955. I was three years old that year. It also suggested family connections that I couldn't quite place. That I held omniscient awareness of the murder was descriptive of my life at the moment, sensing a trauma without full knowledge or confirmation of what had happened. Yet I persistently discounted and rationalized my dreams, accusing myself of creating dreams to justify the flashback as a magnificent attention- getting scheme. I seemed to regard my unconscious as a devious, attention-hungry trickster who enjoyed playing a sick game with me.

In addition to my struggle with denial, another handicap to my straightforward progression in therapy was that I couldn't create a consensus among my various ego states as to the safety or necessity of working in therapy with Edward. Tomboy especially felt threatened. The gist of her sentiment was that she'd done an adequate job of protecting the Hurt Child, so who needed Edward anyway? And what job would she have if Edward became the protector? Discounting Mother and Unaware Father were afraid of being blamed for what happened (if anything had). They didn't want to work with Edward either.

The Hurt Child, more than anyone, yearned for more contact with Edward. For the first time in many years, she had felt both visible and seen. Despite the well of grief that had been tapped, she believed he could be the vehicle to restoration. Five days after the workshop, this entry was made in my journal:

When I close my eyes
I can feel the warmth and support of your hands,
Cradling my heart.
I hear your voice, the tone,
the rhythm, not so much the words. I sense your breath.
I feel excruciating pain, with comfort and
soothing warmth all in the same moment.

If I were to remain split for a lifetime,
I wouldn't give
up the experience of Heartwood.

Disagreement about Edward's role in healing raged, as evidenced by an entry made three days later:

Catastrophic expectations:

> That I will come to trust you (Edward) and let my emotional guard down and be soft and little.
> You will become predatory, attacking, condemning, aggressive, cold, judgmental, and accusing.
> I will experience overwhelming hurt, unmanageable and intolerable. I will depersonalize to the point of inability to function in normal activities.
> I will lose my family. I will develop distrust to the extreme, blocking most
> available sensory awareness out, etc.

My denial and ambivalence over working with Edward in therapy persisted in conj3unction with recurrent symptoms of trauma. After my second session with Edward, I made the following journal entry:

> Figure/ground. Ground seems to be 360° phenomenon.
> Numerous, imposing, demanding black figures. Halloween image.

I felt I was continuously surrounded by menacing, threatening images ready to destroy me at any moment.

Another odd piece to the whole puzzle that presented at roughly the same time all of this was going on was that I was working with a chiropractor, trying to stabilize a scoliosis condition in my spine. (Scoliosis is a condition where the vertebrae assume an S shape rather than stacking straight up, one upon the next.) X-rays of my back and pelvis revealed that I had an asymmetrical pelvis. She described it to me as "twisted," but offered no explanation for the anomaly. I was beginning to connect her finding with the flashback of trauma when some part of me lashed back with vehemence to put down my associations. My journal reads:

It is just as plausible that fearfulness is my basic temperament. My twisted pelvis could have resulted from any sort of insult, including a fall. My sexual inhibition and lack of energy could have resulted from the sex-negative messages thrown at me in puberty. I don't need a more dramatic explanation than this. Stick with the facts.

That journal entry was made at 10:00 p.m., immediately before I went to bed. At 1:50 a.m., I awakened from the following dream:

I am a baby in a crib on Mill Street in Kelso. A man in a white coat, whom I believe is a pharmacist, comes along and begins fondling my genitals. I feel very aroused as he penetrates me with his fingers. He decides he will have intercourse with me and holds my legs apart while trying to force himself into me. I move out of the baby's experience into the pharmacist's and think how good it feels to enter such a small vagina. I have to use a good deal of force, but I make penetration and it is orgasmic.

It turns out this pharmacist has murdered his own grandparents, and the police come to take him away. I am a baby again, in the crib on the street; I can't talk to tell anyone. The sky is growing darker. There is a storm coming and I have no shelter . . .

I woke up in a puddle of menstrual blood, weeks off schedule. Confused about how a pharmacist might be cast in such a sinister role in my dream, the morning following the dream I found the word "pharmacist" in the dictionary. I discovered that the Greek roots of the word are pharmakon (drug, poison) plus poien (to make). Together they mean "to make drugs or poison." I was shocked!! For a moment I was impressed by the ability of my unconscious to use symbols to specify an experience. But the moment passed quickly and my denial returned.

Edward:

Leia had made the commitment from which there is no turning back. Her organismic choice in the workshop was to open to her feelings and to begin in a big way to open to her memories. Ultimately, she could not deny the experience that she had had at the workshop.

In our first therapy session, I felt sad and sober at the prospect of what was to come. I knew that we had only begun, only opened the container of pain that had to be emptied before Leia would be healed.

Leia had functioned well for years, on the surface. She had structured her personality in a manner such that she could handle a certain level of living. She functioned well as long as she was not pushed to another level that called for the presence of more of her person. Her trauma left scars and festering that had to be kept hidden, even from herself, in order to maintain the level of functioning. But when pushed to that level which required more of her person to be present, the damaged part would begin to show.

A way of conceptualizing our task is to think of Leia's personality organization as being pathological because it was not integrated into a functional whole. That is, aspects of her person were split off and hidden away, so to speak. More concretely, her memory was not fully intact (repressed memories), her emotions were not spontaneous (repressed feelings of fear and sadness that would in certain circumstances "leak" out), and her sexuality was inhibited (dulling of pelvic sensations). The task was to remember the split-off memories, express the unexpressed emotions, and re own her full sexuality. These split-off parts left "holes" in her organismic being. But, in order to bring back the split-off aspects, we would first have to take apart this pathological organization. The model is:

Pathological Structure ☐ Destructuring ☐ Healthy Structure

I felt sad and somber knowing that the necessary destructuring meant ineluctable increases of emotional intrusions and cognitive confusion. The repressed would now, with increasing frequency, become manifest. This was the profound difficulty Leia would have. The difficulty I would have would be to support Leia's process, confront, and discourage her understandable doubt, denial, and wish to avoid the process, and appropriately handle the anger Leia would feel towards me at those times when my presence would encourage her pain and confusion. My faith was that the risk Leia and I were taking was worth the gain; it was, then, a "reasonable risk."

My reminder to Leia was that whatever happened to her was literally over; she had survived it and whatever ripples of it she would experience, no matter how bad they felt, could never be as awful as what she had already survived.

We typically ended our sessions with a hug. This was important, I believe, as a repeated experience for Leia of respectful, non-sexual, affectionate, adult touching. Whenever one has a history of disrespectful touch, which has been traumatic, the realm of touch has been tainted for that person. My view is that a complete therapy for this person must involve the use of emotionally corrective, healing touch. Hugging goodbye seemed to be structured enough, being a culturally recognized greeting and parting gesture, and brief enough to be a safe presentation of appropriate touch in our therapy. In addition, we had a history of hugging in our supervisory relationship.

The dream that Leia reported having had the day following our first therapy appointment was a lovely validation of her workshop flashback. Dreams prefer the language of images over the language of words, so Leia's "dreamer" showed her a 1955 Chevrolet, rather than telling her in cold prose that she was three years old when the "bloody" family event happened.

Leia's poem, written five days after the workshop, bears testimony to the potency of body-oriented therapeutic technique applied with presence and compassion. It is impossible to know how very important the body memory was for Leia throughout her ensuing therapy: "I can feel the warmth and support of your hands, cradling my heart." Could words alone have ever been enough to support her through the pain and confusion that was to come?

For some time, Leia vacillated between belief in her own experience of the workshop and her subsequent confirmational experiences and, on the other hand, her doubt and denial. This back-and-forth movement of knowing and denying is to be expected when uncovering repressed memories, and Leia struggled mightily in this. It is greatly to Leia's credit that she showed such persistence in her process, in spite of periods of denial. There was an undeniable integrity in the organismic process in which Leia was engaged, and she would not give up. So, when she was consciously most in denial, her organism would shock her back to her deeper knowing. A beautiful example of such shock is her dream of rape by the "pharmacist," complete with her body's bleeding forth.

6
CHAPTER

I have seriously deliberated as to why it was so difficult for me to believe I had experienced sexual trauma, and my musings have given me this. At three, like all children, I believed I was unconditionally, intrinsically worthy of all the love and attention my world had to give. I lived in the normal childhood bliss of narcissism that is every child's birthright and natural developmental state, in the absence of abuse or neglect. To accept that someone, anyone, could have so little regard for my well-being or happiness as to willingly inflict personal injury of any kind could only mean that I had been wrong in believing I was lovable according to my three-year-old logic. To admit that someone would deliberately violate me as a tiny child could only mean that I wasn't viewed by others as precious. If I wasn't precious, then I must be flawed and unlovable. The pain of feeling unworthy or undeserving of love was too great to admit openly to myself or to anyone else.

And so, despite the raped-baby dream, my denial persisted along with other symptoms, including extreme changes in my menstrual cycle, suicidal fantasies, and panic attacks on therapy day. Despite my symptoms I was insistent with Edward that nothing had happened and that this was all a purely neurotic invention designed to get attention. I didn't want him to see, nor did I want to experience, how ashamed and unlovable I felt myself to be. I developed an obsession with knowing Edward to the greatest extent possible. I acquired nearly everything he had written and poured over the material trying to discover something he'd said or written with which I could disagree or use to justify ending therapy. My motivation was to reject him before he could discover how unlovable I was and reject me. Internally I was warring. Part of me wanted to trust him and move emotionally closer. Other parts wanted simply to flee.

My level of functioning had improved within a few weeks after the workshop. However, psychotherapy sessions continued to be excruciating. I would climb into my car for the drive to Edward's office, looking forward to seeing Edward, and as I drove my hands would begin to tremble and my mouth would become dry. Pulling into the parking lot, I would experience a queasy stomach and constricted breathing. Merely raising the handle to open the car door seemed to require sheer force of will. Once in the waiting room I would experience an urgent impulse to bolt and run, to get back into the car, and speed away. Edward would calmly greet me and my panic would seem terribly out of place. I would help myself to a glass of water to keep my mouth moistened enough to speak during the session. For several successive sessions I felt I couldn't proceed without sitting for several minutes focusing on my breathing to quell my anxiety enough to discuss even casual topics.

Edward was always very patient and accepting. Neither of us understood the reason for my apparent terror, considering I had known Edward for so long and had never before been frightened with him. He had done nothing whatsoever to arouse my fear.

One appointment was an impressive example to me of how connected my terror was to the process of therapy. I was scheduled to be the speaker on a radio talk show on the same day as my therapy appointment. I arrived for therapy that morning and Edward commented on my professional attire. I was able to tell him of my celebrity appearance but subsequently struggled the remainder of the session to speak even short phrases of two syllable words. When we hugged goodbye Edward said gently, "I'm struck by the way your grown-up, professional self can step in and carry on." Once out of the door, my speech returned and later that day as the guest speaker on a talk show, I was completely at ease, spontaneously answering questions with a confident and authoritative demeanor.

The explanation as to why therapy was so terrifying came within weeks. One day I was trying to tell Edward something about the presumed traumatic event when a short phrase broke through my regular conversation in mid-sentence: "I can't do this." Edward responded immediately, stopping me abruptly, and asked, "What is it you can't do?" My mind drew a blank. Confused by my own behavior I offered, "I can't talk," but the words were invented and I knew they weren't completely true. Not knowing what was true, I attempted no further explanation.

When I left his office and was safely seated in my own car, I regressed to the level of a tiny child, wrapped my arms around me, and rocked back and forth, perseverating on the phrase, I can't do this, I can't do this! I experienced bloody threatening intrusive images, as an adult part of me queried, Baby, what is it you can't do? No answer. The rocking eventually subsided. The answer finally came that night. At two o'clock in the morning I was awakened from sleep with an announcement inside my head, I can't tell you what happened. If I tell you I'll be killed. I got out of bed and went to the kitchen to record the revelation in my journal.

The nocturnal message was monumental in that so much of my previously misunderstood behavior, which had seemed so irrational, suddenly made complete sense. Someone had threatened to kill me if I told something, presumably associated with the flashback. Going to therapy to try to make myself feel better meant talking about things that had hurt me. Telling the painful secret was necessary in order to be finished with what was hurting me, and to tell meant the certainty of death in my childhood mind. At last! I could understand why I had felt so threatened in my previous therapy, why I hated Chuck's tape recorder, why I couldn't tell Morgan the dream, and why my physical signs of terror increased as therapy progressed.

I sat at the kitchen table and grieved over my discovery, even though I was relieved to have made it. My grief was that I had spent thirty-five years of my life unconsciously engineering schemes to keep myself and others from knowing some long-dead perverse secret. I'd made life-altering decisions based on the holding of the threat. I'd chosen my marriage partner in part because he didn't seem particularly interested in knowing the core of me. I had always fled suitors who seemed too attentive or too scrutinizing, who might make accurate guesses as to my inner workings. My choice of career was doubtless an effort on my part to figure out how to heal myself without having to reveal the secret or the threat to another. I grieved as I gradually began to comprehend just how much of my life's energy had been spent on guarding a secret, which I, myself, still didn't fully understand, neither what it was nor who was involved. And I grieved for the tiny child within me who had been forced to assume responsibility for her own life and death at an age when such concepts couldn't possibly have been clearly understood. I sat at the table while the rest of my family slept, and I quietly wept and wept until the front of my gown was soaked with my own tears.

It was becoming increasingly difficult to logically argue against the idea of sexual assault. I knew that the collapse of my denial was an essential part of my healing, but as I experienced a dissolution of my defenses I was faced with the next layer of pain, which was a combination of shame and sorrow. If I had to admit that someone had deliberately threatened and hurt me, then I had to admit that someone perceived me as not being lovable enough to merit protection and care. The realization was devastating, and I drifted into a psychological space once more of wanting to die. I began entertaining suicidal thoughts and impulses.

My relationship with Edward became stormy for several weeks while I tried to decide what to do and how to protect myself. The child part of me could see no reason to go on in a world that found her unlovable. I was honestly frightened for my safety. Unlike my life's situation when I was in treatment with Chuck, I now had two children and my death would represent a horrendous tragedy in their lives. I felt out of control some of the time and didn't trust myself not to harm myself. In my more rational moments, I devised a suicide-protection plan that was nothing more than a list of friends I could talk with to help me avert hurting myself. I approached Edward and asked if he would be willing to be called if I had a suicidal crisis. He paused for a moment before answering that he would be willing to be included. I immediately interpreted his pause as a sign that he didn't want to be available and that he was affirming the well-established truth that I was unlovable and undeserving of protection. In the nearly two years I had known him, I'd never telephoned him inappropriately and I was disappointed and angry that he had to stop and consider whether he should be part of my self-protection plan. I had hoped his response would be immediate and spontaneous. I was hurt but too vulnerable to reveal my feelings in that session. Discussing the interaction one week later, I learned that his perception of the flow of communication and mine were quite different. He was scarcely aware that he'd taken any time to consider my request. I was apparently hypersensitive and presumptuous in my evaluation of his behavior. The incident further revealed the nature of my self-concept. I recorded in my journal:

Protection is an illusion. I don 't believe I have protection in any real sense. What I yearn for is the feeling of being valued enough by another to be worth the illusion.

As an adult I can view events that happen to me in a circumscribed manner. An event or interaction is nothing more than what it is. But, to the mind of a child, events and interactions are imbued with everlasting significance and meaning. As an adult, I don't feel the necessity of having everyone's love in order to justify my existence. I have my work and creative expression to bring me feelings of worth, pleasure, and accomplishment. But at three I had no awareness or thoughts of lifelong ambition. The only conceivable purpose I could see for life itself was to share love with those around me. To be unlovable to anyone meant I was completely unlovable. To be unlovable meant my existence was threatened. I didn't have the psychological or cognitive strategies developed to partition this trauma experience off from my overall self-concept. Operating from this early belief system, my life became a process of hiding the shameful truth, as I saw it, so that I could continue to live. I carried the belief that if anyone really knew me, that person would find me to be disgusting and repulsive. My survival strategy, then, was not to let anyone really know me.

My shame-filled self-concept was exposed and evident in my interaction with Edward. Not long after the nocturnal discovery of the threat, I risked discussing what I believed were the characteristics of the alleged perpetrator, based on the dream segments and impressions from the flashback. The discussion evolved into my disclosing body phenomenon and sexual numbing. In a natural way, Edward wove into our dialogue a clear statement that he would never be sexually interactive with me. I froze. I didn't understand why he was telling me this. I was glad we were near the end of our session because my consciousness was fixated on his statement, and I could think of nothing more to say.

The psychologist part of me knew that Edward was saying what we psychologists have been told to say to the survivors of sex abuse. It has become almost a standard of practice for therapists working with sex abuse to make such declarations to their clients.

I would like to briefly explain how we clinicians often arrive at these standards of practice. A newly discovered epidemic, sex abuse, had very few specialists when it first came to light. Nobody had much experience in the field, and those who had seen a few cases flounced into the spotlight to offer workshops instructing others with less experience in how to treat sex abuse survivors. In the absence of clinical research, "specialists" offered common sense treatment strategies that sounded reasonable, and thus, were regularly repeated at professional workshops until they became the standard of practice, often with no more thought than that. I remember attending a weekend workshop on the treatment of adult survivors of sex abuse, and the presenters were adamant that clinicians must "always tell sex abuse clients that you will not be sexual with them."

In my own practice, I almost never tell my sex abused clients that I won't be sexual with them unless there is some reason for me to believe our therapeutic relationship is becoming sexualized. To do so seems to me to be utterly presumptuous and insulting to the client. As with the parenting of my children, my actions convey the message. I can only imagine my sons would think I'd lost my mind if I reminded them periodically that I won't interact with them sexually. They would correctly question my sanity and wonder where on Earth I got the idea they wanted to be sexual with me. What a confusing message! I am not seductive with my clients (or children), and my actions speak for themselves. In this way, I model appropriate boundaries without suggesting anything that might threaten the feelings of worth of the client.

Likewise, I hadn't been seductive with Edward, and I couldn't generate an understanding of what I might have done to make him think I believed he would try to be sexual with me. The statement introduced unnecessary projection, suspicion, and confusion into our interaction.

I knew Edward's intent was to reassure me that he would not try to violate or take advantage of me. (He probably had attended the same workshops as I had.) But what the child in me heard was that he thought of me as disgusting and repulsive, that he couldn't imagine anyone interacting sexually with a shamed and damaged trash heap like me. Instead of feeling reassured and protected, I felt affirmed in my belief that I had no right to exist, that I was human scum. I grieved the entire week until I could meet with him again and tell him the impact his statement had made upon me.

I sobbed, choked, and stuttered through our next session when I described to him what his statement had meant to me. It was a critical point in my treatment with him and, to make matters worse, I wasn't convinced our relationship would survive. I had ended unproductive and abusive therapy relationships in the past and knew I would do so again if this issue was not successfully resolved. I knew it would be self-sabotaging to let the statement pass because I would be stuck on that point until it was addressed.

Edward listened quietly with a look of combined concern and perplexity. I can characterize his successful defusing of the situation more by what he didn't do than by what he did. He didn't argue with me or suggest my feelings were stupid. He didn't become defensive and try to make me responsible for what he'd said. He didn't suggest that my behavior had provoked his comment. He didn't say, "There, there, Honey, it's all right," patronizing me, or tell me how glad he was that I could bring it to him. He listened, and he seemed to genuinely study the situation from inside of him, as though his own awareness was expanding. He apologized in an honest, rather than groveling manner. He agreed with me, that I had never behaved suggestively with him, validating my perception and restoring a fragment of my self-respect. The session ended well, with our having strengthened our bond rather than creating a schism.

I learned several valuable lessons in that experience. I was reminded of the danger of creating unyielding rules, practices, or techniques and applying them to all clients of a given category, assuming each needs the same thing. I can imagine that it could be therapeutic to tell a client who sexualized most relationships that the therapy relationship would be different. But to assume all sex abused clients have the same needs or reactions to the abuse is, at the very least, prejudicial.

I also learned the beneficial potential contained in mistakes if handled well. What came to light for me through Edward's blunder was the extreme damage that had been leveled at my core self-concept by the abuse. Had he been the perfect therapist I might not have plummeted to the germinal issue, perhaps ever. And the fact that we could reconcile taught me that nothing has to be viewed as absolute, unless we so choose. I could be angry and hurt, and express those feelings without the end result being the loss of love and care. I had at last discovered one of the templates for my healing.

As my relationship with Edward stabilized, my unconscious continued to offer possibilities for revealing the perpetrator. I vacillated between wanting to know and not wanting to know who it might be. What if the perpetrator was my father? Could I stand the pain of such extreme betrayal? I entered a bargaining phase in which I told myself I could accept knowing so long as it was a stranger or even a distant relative. I didn't want the perpetrator to be someone close to me, and I dreaded further pursuit of answers out of fear of what I might discover.

My dreams continued to offer a metaphorical description of my perception of my search for truth. I wrote in my journal:

I am being pulled by an unseen force through total darkness toward the answer. I know I am now a thin line away when there is a sudden charge, almost like an explosion, and I am awake.

Several days later, I recorded the following dream:

Again, I am awakened with a knowing about denial, implosion, and the death layer. To fully accept the disgrace of childhood incest is in complete contradiction with the self as I know it; to be drawn into blackness, total nothingness (death), and blasted out the other side (rebirth). Fear of the unknown. Can this be survived? Is there life on the other side?

It was apparent that on an existential level my unconscious viewed the process I had entered as a life-or-death situation. The more willing I was to know the truth, without setting conditions as to who would be an acceptable perpetrator to discover, the more willing was my unconscious to offer clues. At 1:50 a.m., roughly seven weeks after the initial flashback, I awakened with a message from my unconscious. My journal entry reads:

The answer to the question "who done it" resides in the right arm and both ankles. The sense I am given is one of foreboding. Proceed with caution. Move with strength, but don't rush it. Pain lies ahead. This isn't easy. Do one at a time. Right arm first. Not a job for a sissy.

The nocturnal revelation was complete with two detailed anatomical charts; one showing a human figure with a triangle drawn from a point in the center of the forehead to both ankles, forming a perfect isosceles triangle; the second chart showing a triangle originating from the right arm connecting to both ankles, roughly forming a right triangle. The dream message was that the first triangle represented ideal balance; the second represented my current condition.

The following morning I grabbed my dictionary to find the root of isosceles, trying to learn what the dream meant. I found that isosceles meant having two equal sides, and also that the Greek root, isoskeles, was the root of the word scoliosis, the condition where the spine is crooked, with which I was afflicted.

I remembered the chiropractor had explained to me that I probably developed scoliosis as a result of my pelvis being so misaligned. Since my spine rests on my pelvis, scoliosis could have developed because my pelvis was crooked. Was the dream suggesting that my pelvis had been twisted from the force used to penetrate my once tiny body? The thought sickened me. At the same time, I was grateful to my own persistent unconscious mind for continuing to yield rich information for me to learn about my true self. It was relentless and amazingly consistent in directing me toward an answer.

The healing process of my unconscious mind and requirements for living successfully in the real world came into direct conflict soon after the triangle dream, bringing therapy to a premature end. I had applied for membership to the National Register of Health Service Providers in Psychology. Membership to that organization was required in order for me to have hospital admission privileges. Requirements for membership include one year of post-doctoral supervision by a psychologist or psychiatrist. The additional year of supervision had to be completed within four years of graduation and my time was running out. I received a letter rejecting my application for membership on the basis that my hospital work had been supervised by various medical doctors, not a psychiatrist, and none of my eighteen months of supervision with Edward was accepted because the frequency of our supervision sessions was considered inadequate. The requirement specified a ratio of clinical hours to supervision hours, which we had satisfied, but in reality frequency of meeting was a rigid policy with the agency. Edward wrote a letter on my behalf but the reviewing committee wouldn't budge.

My choices were grim. If I continued therapy, it was possible I would never be admitted to the National Register and I could foresee numerous important ways that my lack of membership could hinder my career. If I stopped therapy in mid-process I might never regain the momentum to find the answers I was seeking. I didn't have the financial resources to pay for both therapy and supervision. The dilemma held deep significance. It represented a choosing between my adult self, complete with responsibility for the financial support of my family, and my own inner child. One choice threatened my future; the other threatened my past. And I couldn't ignore the pathetic irony that the organizational rules of the National Register, now causing me such personal agony, were presumably predicated on protection of mental health consumers.

Edward left the decision to me and I opted to end therapy, only two months after my suicidal ruminations, and three months after the initial flashback. I returned to Edward as my supervisor and hopelessly abandoned my quest for answers. My dream life became correspondingly subdued, but I was far from finished. I continued living a life filled with sorrowful outbursts and episodes of anxiety. Only now I had no one to safely share it with.

Edward:

It was remarkable that Leia could function at such a high level professionally while feeling such terror and confusion at times. She was very skillful at shifting out of her terrified child ego state into a competent adult ego state or parent ego state in order to engage in her professional activities or take care of her children. At times, when not involved in either of these areas, and when she came to see me, she switched into a child ego state. This shift was, of course, essential when she came for therapy. It was the child in her who needed to be heard, seen, understood, and healed.

When working with someone I listen carefully for such telling intrusions as Leia's "I can't do this." To take such a short phrase that breaks through as important is to honor that inner child. By letting her know that I heard her, I was encouraging the child part to go on and say more. She did say more, so much more, that night. What she revealed was her "catastrophic expectation," that belief that threatened an awful punishment if she continued to remember and reveal her story, eventually revealing her assailant. For her to become aware of her catastrophic expectation gave her an understanding of much of her previous perplexing behavior.

The incident of my "blunder" is a beautiful example of how much more basic genuine humanistic respect is than techniques in the therapeutic process. I could never have planned or engineered a technical intervention that could have brought us to this deeper level of trust and mutual respect. This was, to use a phrase that was popular some years ago, a critical incident in psychotherapy. It happened without plan or forethought, indeed starting with a blunder on my part. We were able, fortunately, to make use of the blunder and to take advantage of the opportunity that it presented.

With our relationship solid and deepened, Leia's dreamer continued to offer her material, carefully timed and regulated so as not to overwhelm, but to keep the process of discovery and assimilation moving. Perhaps Leia had now found the source of her scoliosis.

Having done all that either of us could think to do, Leia accepted the predicament that she was in with the National Register. She came to a difficult decision. I believed that this would be a delay in healing, a temporary hiatus, but that she had too much integrity and spunk to be stopped for long.

7
CHAPTER

$\mathcal{M}$y supervision with Edward was now mildly awkward for two reasons, the first being our mutual awareness of the untimely arbitrary disruption of therapy. I was left with unfocused, unexpressed despair about the unfairness of the situation. The National Register is a large and complex bureau, and I knew the futility of trying to satisfy my need for understanding from "them." I had no one who understood the situation well to turn to, and it would have been misuse of supervision time to discuss it further with Edward.

The second reason I felt we had become a bit of an awkward match was that, by now, I had developed a strong specialization in health psychology with a greater knowledge base in my area than most other local psychologists, including Edward. I worked with clients experiencing life-threatening disease, and I had done so for three years, both in a hospital setting and in private practice. I was medically trained as a nurse and worked as a volunteer AIDS instructor for the Red Cross. I also taught an overview of Alzheimer's disease for the Alzheimer's Association. I was conducting research on the psychological factors associated with breast cancer, and I had produced several professional publications in my field. I was occasionally featured on radio and television for my expert opinions.

I knew of no one in my immediate community who was any more knowledgeable in my area of expertise than I. It almost seemed silly to be spending time and energy on supervision when my work as a therapist would have been so much more favorably influenced by stabilizing my intrapsychic life. Edward was quick to admit that I had become the local expert and that he didn't have much to add to my knowledge base. His style of supervision, thankfully, was that of focusing on the person of the therapist, which didn't require his exceeding my expertise. Although his knowledge of health psychology was admittedly limited, he could advise me on practice issues and self-management in the therapy hour, so that became the focus of our supervision relationship. A portion of my practice was with well clients, and I could present case material from them and get meaningful feedback, as well.

Our interaction abruptly shifted from a deeply personal, energetic, living experience to a more lackluster, lifeless academic exercise. I was trapped in my pain, which was the pain of abandonment, and the pain was magnified by my being in the presence of the one person who could help me, while essentially being forbidden to ask for the help I needed. I was struck by the apparent repetition in adulthood of what had happened to me as a child. I'd been injured as a small child and, because of the threat of death, was left with no one but myself to take care of me. I had been a child, taking care of a child, and now I was doing it once again, except I was wearing a bigger body, pretending real hard to be a grown-up.

Edward seemed sad to me. Perhaps it was my projection, but it seemed to me that he felt almost as helpless as I did. I know, as a parent, the feeling of caring for a sick or injured child, wanting for nothing more than to bring pain to an end, and the feeling of helplessness and frustration that comes when I am ineffective in doing so. I needed to believe that Edward felt that way about me. I hoped he shared my sadness, even though it was pointless and contrary to rules for us to talk.

A few weeks after the transition back to supervision, Edward informed me that he would be conducting a professional training workshop at Esalen Institute in Big Sur, California. He invited me to attend. While he didn't openly predict an opportunity to finish the work we'd begun, I believed his invitation was for that purpose, and I appreciated his thinking of me.

The idea of going to Esalen revealed once more my feelings of low self-worth. In my mind Esalen was a gathering place for famous and important people. George Leonard, Henry Miller, and Fritz Perls were among the elitists who had spent time at Esalen, as had some of the senior members of my graduate school faculty. I felt I was too lowly, too ordinary and unimportant to be comfortable at Esalen. Nevertheless, it was an opportunity to do something about all of the unprocessed information that had been laid out by my unconscious. I decided to go, worthy or not.

I vividly recall the days before my departure from Atlanta for California. I would not allow myself the luxury of a fantasy of what Esalen might be like. I was afraid that I would become apprehensive and cancel the trip. When thoughts or images began to surface I quickly distracted myself, knowing that other aspects of my personality were not as eager to search out truth as I was.

Finally, the day of departure came. The flight to California was a terrible struggle. Once the door of the jet airplane closed and opportunities for escape were eliminated, all of the feelings of fear and apprehension I had been suppressing pressed forth for acknowledgment. My anxiety mounted without restraint until my very thoughts grew clouded. I felt physically weak and nauseated. The back of my head and neck burned and tingled, as it had in the days following the Heartwood workshop, signaling uncontrolled dissociation. I could scarcely keep my eyes open to maintain the thin thread of attachment I held to reality by way of vision. Vague images housing dire predictions floated in and out of my consciousness during the long plane ride. By the time I arrived in San Francisco I was exhausted from the effort it had taken to appear normal on the outside with so much turmoil on the inside.

My personal suffering, however, long and tense as it had been, receded in the background the moment I entered the rustic and spectacular beauty of the Esalen Complex. I instantly understood Esalen's attractiveness to the exceptionally creative members of our species. I arrived late in the afternoon and the day was perfect, with a sky that was bright and cloudless. Esalen is perched on the cliffs of Big Sur, overlooking the Pacific Ocean. The sound of the breakers on the rocks at the ocean's edge makes a soothing sensual background for the magnificent beauty of the complex. The environment alone had an immediate calming effect on my soul. The monarch butterflies had migrated to this location, and the gathering of so many in one place provided an uplifting distraction from my personal pain.

The workshop attendees gathered for the first time in the rustic meeting room on Sunday evening. I was relieved that there were only seven of us. The meeting itself pushed me back into the pain I had escaped for a few hours while enjoying the Esalen scenery. I knew what I was here for, and I was both miserable and terrified. The misery was greater than the terror, and I was ready to do nearly anything it might take to make me feel better.

Edward introduced the topic of Embodied Gestalt Practice, describing the philosophy and underlying principles while my own attention floated from me to him, then back to me. When he finished his introduction, he asked that each member of the group introduce themselves and state what each hoped to gain over the week. I was the last to speak. I rehearsed in my mind many different possibilities of what I could say while the others were speaking. My emotions were much too close to the surface by the time it was finally my turn to speak. I was afraid to say much because tears were already burning my eyes, and I didn't want my first introduction to be perceived by the group as how utterly vulnerable I was. Much like a wounded animal, my tendency was to withdraw and cower. I simply said my name and added, "I'd like to find some peace." Edward gave me an understanding nod and said nothing. The others seemed to look at me with questions in their eyes and I felt little strength to respond. Before we finished for the evening, Edward asked that we observe our dreams and try to remember them, and to return the next morning ready to begin.

I spent a restless, tormented night with little sleep. I dreamed, but was unable to carry the dream content from sleep into wakeful consciousness. However, the lyrics of two different popular songs were playing in my mind when I awoke and I was able to capture them.

One set of lyrics was, "I'm gonna harden my heart, I'm gonna swallow my tears, I'm gonna turn and leave." It didn't take much scholarly thought to establish an interpretation of those lyrics. My unconscious was clearly struggling with resistance. The second set was, "I can't tell you why, no, I can't tell you why." Again, the message was obvious. Parts of me were resistant and terrified to work on the issues that had been exposed. It was a sad dilemma. I couldn't retreat into ignorance and denial; too much had transpired for me to pretend nothing had ever happened. To move forward seemed the most terrifying thing I could possibly imagine. And I was stuck in between the known and the fear of the unknown.

When the group reconvened Monday morning, Edward invited descriptions of dreams and I shared what had surfaced for me. He invited me to the center of the room to initiate Gestalt dialogue between the part of me that wanted to work and the angry, defiant part of me that didn't. He asked that I give the defiant part a name on the spot. For a moment nothing came to mind, then surprisingly, with a sudden force came the announcement "Diana." Under Edward's direction I openly interacted with this aspect of myself, who was exceedingly stubborn, proud, and haughty.

Edward gave me the assignment to spend some portion of the next twenty-four hours negotiating with Diana for information and permission to work. He went on to work with others in the group and I remained with my thoughts, observing others but feeling self-absorbed and preoccupied.

When the morning session was concluding, the group began to interact playfully and various members, including Edward, proceeded to wrestle like cub bears on the floor in the center of the carpeted room. I watched from a distance but made no effort to join the frolic. I vaguely felt I'd lived this scene before. I remembered being a child, watching my adult cousin, Jack, wrestle with the children in the family. I remembered feeling that I wanted to wrestle and play too, but for some reason I had held myself back, feeling sad and left out. Observing the present interaction triggered something for me and later that day I wrote in my journal:

I have a wide variety of faces transferred onto Edward. I experience attraction and fear all at once. I have the impression of children, all playing with a male grown-up, and I'm away from the group, watching and yearning to be a part, yet knowing that I cannot because the price I would pay for such simple pleasure is much too high. I seem to hold the belief that I am the one. The others are not in danger, but I am.

I spent the rest of the day in my own thoughts, watching Edward work with others, and feeling doubtful that I would learn anything from the defiant Diana. I was concerned that the week would pass uneventfully, and I would be no further ahead than when I arrived at Esalen.

The group reconvened Tuesday morning and I'd spent another restless night that yielded no more information. I had the suspicion that I was shutting down internally, unconsciously making myself go numb, and that this was to be Diana's answer—stubborn resistance.

Edward began this session by instructing on the connection of breath to psychological experience. He invited the group to participate in a hands-on demonstration, working in pairs with one another, to practice various techniques for using breath to uncover blocked experiences. He very pointedly asked me if I felt comfortable in doing so, and I agreed that I did, although I was feeling shaky and vulnerable. Better that I should continue to experience whatever might come than go dead, I reasoned.

A young man from Denmark, named Ken, chose me to be his partner. I practiced various techniques taught by Edward on him, which involved training him in diaphragmatic breathing, and then massaging his diaphragm to soften physical restrictions to breath. Then it was my turn for him to practice on me.

Edward was circulating around the room assisting the pairs of people in executing the techniques properly. Again he stopped and pointedly asked, "Are you sure you want to do this?" I'd made it through the first part of the exercise, practicing the technique on my partner, and he had been fine. He'd actually asked that I apply more pressure. The exercises didn't seem particularly threatening, so again I said, "Yes, I'm fine." I noted and deeply appreciated Edward's protectiveness.

Ken and I proceeded in the exercises. First, I breathed into my upper chest, to experience the breath pattern associated with physical labor or excitation. Then I practiced diaphragmatic breathing, the breath of relaxation, drawing in breath from my lower abdomen. All was well. I felt relatively calm, yet at the same time an increasing awareness of profound sadness was perceptible, and I questioned my ability to contain. I considered withdrawing but decided that to do so would be awkward. I would appear, and feel, cowardly, and my partner would have nobody to practice with. I tried to convince myself that I had the strength to continue without serious difficulty.

The final exercise was diaphragmatic massage, which required me to breathe deeply while my partner, during exhalation, pressed his fingers in and upward at the edge of my ribs to massage my diaphragm. It was not painful but was mildly uncomfortable. He started in the middle of my body, near what is called the xiphoid process, and worked outward toward my waist, first on one side, then the other. I wasn't disturbed by the work near the center of my body, but as he progressed toward my waist I felt agitated, scared, and frantic. I attempted to calm myself. The exercise was nearly over. I repeatedly reassured myself mentally that I could manage until it was over; I persevered on the thought that I had the necessary strength.

Ken had completed the exercise on my left side first. Only the right side remained. My partner was completing the diaphragmatic massage from the center, as instructed, working his fingers toward my right side. I was concentrating as hard as I possibly could on my breathing, trying to hold on long enough to complete the exercise, desperately trying to fend off something horrible that I couldn't identify. As his fingers moved closer to my waist, my tension mounted, and my concentration broke. He touched a particular point on my right side and my consciousness was instantly flooded with confusion. Tears gushed forth, streaming down the sides of my face. My breath became rapid and instantly moved into my upper chest. My fretfulness transformed into terror. I was thrashing my head from side to side. My partner sat back from me and watched what was happening.

Edward called to me from across the room where he'd been coaching other participants, "Leia, are you all right?" I tried to raise my head. My entire body stiffened from head to toe. My legs rolled inward toward one another, and became locked so tight as to be immediately painful. And in a raw, unrestrained cry, I heard myself answer, "I'm in pain!" The anguish in my voice was unmistakable.

A wild and terrifying image of me as a very little girl running in the woods with someone, a man with a hat, stalking me had flashed into my consciousness. He grabbed me by the waist and my consciousness was instantly behind the man. I knew he had my body but that I was not in it.

Edward must have flown across the room, for he appeared instantly. I was sobbing uncontrollably, and my body was shaking with the sounds forcing their passage through my throat. Edward turned me onto my left side and drew my legs up toward my chest; he then molded my head downward with his right arm so that I was in a fetal position. My arms automatically pulled in and crossed, covering my heart. He positioned himself on the floor beside me and covered my head and upper body with his arms, as though shielding me from incoming artillery on a battlefield.

I have no idea how long I wept, but what has remained prominent in my memory is the sensory experience: the warmth of Edward's arms, the feel of his breath, the sound of his voice as he passed a tissue to me. I have never felt so completely protected from danger as in those few minutes. Gradually, as my sobbing subsided, other members of the group cautiously pressed closer to where Edward and I were huddled together on the floor. Ken laid down behind me, and with Edward to my front and Ken behind I was enfolded in human warmth. My sobbing stopped and started again and again with the intervals of peace growing longer each time until, at last, my sobbing stopped altogether. Somewhere between sobs I was aware of Edward thanking Diana for delivering her information. For the first time in an unknown length of time, I felt total peace. Fear subsided and was replaced by an intense desire to sleep.

Other workshop members were becoming playful and crawled onto the three of us to form a pile of human bodies. My energy spent, I couldn't match the joyfulness of my peers, but I did feel a deep sense of satisfaction, peace, and appreciation for those around me, although I wanted to be left alone. The remainder of the afternoon I spent on the rocks at the ocean's edge, watching the rhythmic motion of the breakers in a sort of mindless tranquility.

The peacefulness I experienced following the flashback at Esalen marked the beginning of the end to the pervasive anxiety, confusion, and dissociation I'd known in the previous months. Now that the assault was known, my thoughts gradually shifted from the struggle over whether or not something had happened, to a quest to find meaning in my suffering, which seemed, on first inspection, to be utterly meaningless.

As a little girl, I had so often heard from my deeply religious, adoring Grandmother Hanson, "If it's meant to be, it will be." That sentiment came back to me in the days after the flashback. I wondered how a perpetrator can justify violent sexual acts toward children, towards me. Was it "meant to be" as my grandmother suggested? Could one orgasmic moment be worth the ruthless and bloody violation of a tiny child? And, had I benefited in some way from this seemingly senseless trauma? I couldn't find any method of thinking that could help me understand a perpetrator, and instead of feeling upset and terrified as in the previous months, I felt sort of in awe at how bizarre the entire experience had seemed. In some ways the rape had influenced my entire life, and I knew I would never have absolute closure without knowing something about my attacker. I also knew the probability of gaining valid information was exceedingly slim, given that nobody from my family could recollect a single suspicious moment from my childhood. My focus shifted from the assault to a yearning to know or understand my assailant. I reasoned that if I had an awareness of who he was and what he was like, meaning could be discerned from all of this. Without information I felt lost with regard to the future. How was I to proceed from here?

It is a natural human inclination to convert tragedy into triumph, at least for some, and so it was for me. I wanted to unveil some way to comprehend what had happened to me in a manner that would positively contribute to my own life and to others.

The end of the week at Esalen was rapidly approaching. The weather had remained exceptionally beautiful through the week. For our last evening meeting Edward had planned an outdoors sensory awareness exercise. We were given the instruction to begin by following him through the Esalen garden and into the forest path along a stream descending from the coastal mountains. We were to walk slowly, without conversing with one another, and we were to take time to examine and touch whatever struck our fancy. The idea, I believe, was to rediscover the pleasure and wisdom of our senses, which we all generally ignore for the purpose of conducting the business of our daily lives.

We lingered in the garden for a while before following Edward to the rocky stream in the woods where he gave the next set of instructions, which were very simple. He asked that we sit or stand quietly and listen to the sound of the stream over the rocks. We were to allow the stream to speak to us.

I had a moment of resistance to this part of the exercise. Whether I like it or not, I am still a bit of a pragmatist with a scientific bent, and the idea of a creek talking to me seemed like a silly game. The sound was soothing, however, and I spent the time meditating and enjoying my newly discovered peace without straining to hear the voice of the stream. I had learned to take the instructions of workshop leaders and modify them to my own purpose. I knew Edward wouldn't mind.

As I sat with my eyes closed, listening to the rush of the stream over the rocks and envisioning light in my heart, I gradually became aware of the image of four women gathered together to address me. They were: the sharpshooter, Annie Oakley; the first woman doctor, Elizabeth Blackwell; the Goddess Diana; and the Indian guide for the Lewis and Clark expedition, Sacajawea. Sacajawea moved forward from the line of women, and without her speaking, I was filled with "knowing" her simple but profound message. She conveyed to me the necessity of the childhood assault; that it had made me strong. Tears streamed down my face as the truth and elegance of this simple knowing evolved into full recognition within me. I did not resist the sentiment or explanation served up to me. It seemed to fill each and every cell of my body with this irrefutable, absolute truth. I examined it without my usual skepticism, for there was literally no room for doubt in that moment.

The sun was making its descent over the ocean when we started the final exercise, which was to climb down to the short, rocky beach and look carefully at the debris delivered from the ocean. We were instructed to allow an object from nature to "choose" us. Having just communed with four archetypical females, I had very little skepticism about being chosen. It seemed to me that anything could happen if I would allow myself openness to the experience. So I climbed over and around the rock, along with my peers, as the crash of Pacific breakers filled my ears, and I waited to be chosen. I knew what Edward meant about being chosen. I have had the experience of attraction and recognition of an object, event, or person before. It reminded me of shopping and finding just the right something I was looking for and feeling deep contentment. I resolved in this exercise that I wouldn't pick up something just to have it. If I didn't experience the attraction I would be satisfied that nothing was there for me.

I strolled, then lingered here and there for what seemed like a long time without feeling attracted or drawn to anything in particular, and I was preparing to join the group empty-handed. I scanned the rocks beneath my feet for the last time when my eyes struck on the color red. Red seemed so out of place against the blue-gray ocean with white breakers, and the greens and browns of the adjacent forest. But there it was, a black and white stone with a smattering of red that made it stand out from the surrounding bed of broken rock beneath my feet. It seemed lonely among its neighbors because of its dissimilarity. I picked it up and felt it expressed a compact version of my personhood in a way I couldn't begin to express in words.

The group gathered on the rocky beach to discuss and share individual discoveries from each of the three exercises. I tried to describe my tribunal with the four archetypical women and the knowing I had experienced. Then I tried to explain the stone, but my words couldn't seem to do those feelings justice, as is so often the case when elucidating on the symbolic. I said something about the transformation from darkness into light and my experience at Esalen being captured in the lines and regions of the stone that joined the two. The red, I knew, represented blood, which for me meant the essentials of life, and violence, and death. The red of the stone had called to me with a backdrop of black and white. The red had blended the colors of the stone and red had held the passion.

I slipped the stone into my pocket for a journey to Atlanta so that I could continue to ponder its significance for me in the months to come.

We completed the exercise and proceeded up the steep stairs toward the main complex. Ken was walking behind me, and he gently placed his hand on my shoulder as he began softly talking with me about the experience.

"What you got from all of this is exactly what I would have wanted for you to get. You may not yet fully realize what a gift you've been given. That man who assaulted you took a great deal of Karma on himself."

His tender support registered deep within me, and I appreciated his interacting with me on many levels. It was his touch that had facilitated the flashback, and I am certain to never forget the pain and peace I shared with him that week.

My thoughts were turning homeward and I wondered what awaited my discovery in the months ahead.

Edward:

The Esalen workshop provided another "safe emergency" for Leia. As I read Leia's description and conjure up my memories of her work there, I come to the following stream of consciousness: trust the process...be patient...be supportively, non-intrusively, non-demandingly present. That's it! Create a safe setting, use an appropriate technique to launch the process, and then trust the process, be patient, and be supportively, non-intrusively, non-demandingly present.

Once again Leia's body remembered. A seemingly simple touch invited the revealing of repressed memory, the coming forth of a complex of body sensation, emotion, visual image, and body expression from another time.

Body Experience ☐ Emotion ☐ Memory

Following this, I, and later Ken and I, provided and emotionally corrective experience through direct body contact. The peacefulness that ensued was a harbinger of the ending of what Leia called her "pervasive anxiety, confusion, and dissociation."

In the shamanic exercises at Esalen, Leia was "visited" by four spirit women, women who could speak to her with profundity. She "heard" the stream as many ancients have done and knew now that, in her own words, "there was literally no room for doubt in that moment."

8
CHAPTER

My experience at Esalen had catapulted me into exhilaration. I was hungry for information about the four women I had experienced in meditation. Shortly after my return to Atlanta I located books on each one and began a search into their character and personhood, hoping to discover something relevant for me.

I learned that Diana was the Roman Goddess of the moon and of hunting. She was the protectress of women. Sacajawea had been a Shoshone tribeswoman who had been kidnapped as a young girl and made a slave of the French trader, Charbonneau. Through various twists of fate she became an essential component to the success of the Lewis and Clark expedition to the Northwest. Annie Oakley was the highly acclaimed sharpshooter for Bill Cody's Wild West Show in the late 1800s. And Elizabeth Blackwell was the first woman doctor, having triumphed over prejudice against women in the medical field. The trait common to all four was that of stretching out of traditional role expectations to become more. There were many points of contact between my story and theirs. Learning about these women was interesting, and I was fascinated by the way my mind had accurately selected female characters with life processes and ambitions so similar to my own. Yet I felt a nagging sense of being unfinished with what I wanted most to accomplish, that of finding the identity of the perpetrator, and learning exactly what had happened.

I resumed supervision with Edward upon my return to Atlanta, and I felt like I was a horse in a starting gate at a race, waiting for the gun to fire so I could free myself to learn who the perpetrator was. The gate holding me back was, of course, the requirement for supervision held by the National Register of Health Service Providers. I couldn't resume therapy until the requirement was fully satisfied. As the months dragged on, my energy for pursuing information about the perpetrator waned. The waiting process left me aimless and weary. I couldn't return to therapy for nearly eight months after the Esalen trip, and by then the passion for the quest had irretrievably passed. The interim time period seemed to me to be the demise of an opportunity.

I made diligent, conscientious effort to maintain a connection to the healing process during the months of waiting. I journaled religiously and participated in a dream exploration group. I exercised aggressively and trained in long-distance running to try to hold onto the spirit and strength of Diana. I saw a massage therapist to try to awaken my awareness of bodily sensation and pleasure, hoping to access body memories. But, despite my persistent efforts, the parts of me that had once been so energized for healing action gradually atrophied under the burden of slowly passing time and inattention. Edward and I diligently and honestly trudged through supervision sessions, briefly discussing Esalen now and then, and deliberately returning to the task of training. By the time the required months had passed, my energy and money were depleted. I resumed therapy, but it was without focus, and I decreased the frequency of our appointments to conserve money.

I hoped that, given time in therapy, my zest to solve the mystery would return. But it didn't. The opportunity had passed and even a second trip to Esalen in the spring following the completion of supervision in October couldn't resurrect the momentum to learn the truth. I spent my therapy hours in discourse over my present-day interpersonal relationships, pondering professional articles I might write, and enjoying Edward's pleasant company. I gradually reconciled myself to the high probability that I would never know the identity of the perpetrator, as the subject came up less and less often. The cost of not knowing was that an element of denial could linger unchallenged—like the old saying, "Without a corpse there is no murder." I wrestled with the nagging uncertainty that without an identifiable perpetrator or clear memory, there might not really have been an assault. The evidence was still circumstantial and incomplete in my mind. Maybe I had, in truth, made the whole thing up.

On those occasions when I would share my doubt with Edward, he would nearly chuckle at my attempts to undo my awareness, gently shaking his head as if to say, "What will it take to rid your denial?" On one occasion he seemed to lose patience momentarily, and with a slightly raised voice declared, "Leia, there were six other people in the room. We all saw what you were living through. If it was an act, I'd sure like to know where you studied drama, because it was great acting if it isn't true!" I knew he didn't want my denial to gain a new foothold.

The seasons passed and I was contacted about a professional position becoming available in the Northwest, nearer my family of origin. I flew out for an interview and quickly decided the time was right for a homeward move. The educational system was better for my children, and much to my liking, the area was less populated. I wanted our sons to grow up knowing aunts, uncles, and cousins. I'd been in the big city for twenty years and I longed for a less stressful existence. I knew I would miss Edward, but with the rest of my life ahead of me I wouldn't allow my feelings of dependence to stop me. I had gotten more from him than I'd ever expected or bargained for.

We sold property and relocated to Oregon in September. Any concerns I had about sex abuse were superseded by the necessary activities of relocating, learning a new job, and establishing supportive networks for my family in Eugene, Oregon. I was nearly symptom free and was able to function without interference from anxiety or dissociation. I was well on the mend from my experiences, and also, my husband had broken his bondage of alcohol. He reminded me of Rumpelstiltskin, waking up after a long period of sleep, and we needed time to become reacquainted. At last my life was unfolding on an even keel, and I was only remotely and infrequently aware of the pressure of a vague shadow in my consciousness, veiling a perpetrator I now believed I would never be able to identify.

The winter holidays were especially cheerful to anticipate. For the first time in nearly twenty years I lived near enough to my family that I could participate in the festive family reunions. On Christmas Day at the family gathering I finally learned, unexpectedly and in a haphazard fashion, of my being left alone with a family member known to be sexually deviant.

The day of the reunion had been beautiful and brisk. The food was plentiful and delicious. The children playfully raced and tagged outside while the old-timers gathered in the warmth of the cozy living room before a blazing fire to swap stories and share memories. The scene could have been a Rockwell painting. The conversation was upbeat and playful. Laughter thundered through the people-filled house of my older sister where we had all come together. Sex abuse was the farthest thing from my mind as I interacted with relatives I hadn't seen in many years. I laughed and hugged my way through the day in peace and joviality befitting the season.

Conversation slowly died down as the shadows lengthened to announce the coming of evening. People dispersed in small family groups and I exchanged goodbyes and see-you-soons until my own family was among the last to depart. My oldest sister, Connie, was loading her car to leave with her husband and my elderly Aunt Bess. I hugged Aunt Bess before she climbed into the back seat and adjusted herself for comfort. I had offered another "I love you, I'm so glad you came, "when she looked up at me from her seat and asked, "Do you remember the time you spent the night at my house and you got scared in the middle of the night and Jack carried you down the stairs, screaming your head off?" Her eyes locked with mine. My breath stopped with the instant internal recognition of what she was saying. Innocently, without her apparent knowledge, she disclosed the single piece of conclusive information that had eluded me for the many years of my therapy. My denial seemed to rush through a swirling vortex—it was real! The flashbacks weren't childhood inventions designed to gain attention. Yes, it was all undeniably real.

My parents had told me some fifteen years prior about Bess's son, Jack, who had violated one of my older sisters when she was three. He was babysitting her while my mother bid farewell to my father, who was going overseas during World War II. My parents had never told Aunt Bess what her son had done. He was thirteen at the time, and they apparently believed he would outgrow the behavior and that nothing more would happen.

Mentally returning to the present, I shook my head. "No," I muttered in response to her question, wondering if I was telling the truth. After all, flashbacks aren't really memories, I reasoned. I studied her face as she studied mine. I perceived a combination of threat and curiosity, and I looked carefully for a sign of deeper disclosure. I wondered if she knew or suspected that Jack had hurt me, but I couldn't discern if there was more information that she was holding back. Why had the event made such an impact on her that she would remember it thirty-seven years later?

"How old was I?" I asked, forcing the words through constricted vocal chords.

"You couldn't have been more than three," she replied. "I don't remember why you were staying with me."

Our conversation was interrupted by the completion of car loading and readiness for departure by my oldest sister. I stood in the driveway absorbed in my own thoughts and feelings, and waved mechanically as they drove off.

My thoughts and emotions were mixed and opposing. Part of me was elated at the final verification of trauma. I wasn't crazy and I never had been. The information Aunt Bess had handed me snapped into place like the interlocking piece of a jigsaw puzzle. Her upstairs bedrooms had the slanted ceilings of the roofline, with a window at the far end. My age had been three, the year 1955. Her son was known by my parents to be a pedophile. I'd been "screaming my head off," as a child would do in pain.

The one shred of doubt I had held throughout all of therapy had survived, predicated on the premise that no one in my immediate family could recall a single time I'd been left unsupervised with anyone they felt could possibly be of a suspicious nature. That doubt was dashed in the space of one brief sentence, and I was liberated. My unconscious had not lied to me. It had delivered its recollection of trauma systematically and deliberately, despite my tenacious denial.

I thought, for a moment, how utterly sick it seemed on the surface, to be thrilled at learning I'd been left with a pedophile who had hurt me. The entire drama, start to finish, still seems sick to me. But, to the tiny child still living in me, I could no longer abandon her in ignorance. A pedophile doesn't generally outgrow the sexual practice without deliberate and intentional effort. Jack, as I knew him and as others had described him, would not have allowed an opportunity to gratify his perverse desires to pass. He would have savagely seized the chance alone with me as he had done with my sister. I have worked with, and studied pedophilia, and I have a knowledge base as to the patterns of associated behavior. No further doubt would survive the query and revelation of Aunt Bess.

My mind was spinning in January with the question of what to do with this new information. I felt an urgency to contact Aunt Bess to see if she could or would tell me anything more. Closer family members were somewhat discouraging about the probability of Aunt Bess volunteering any additional information because she tended to be a guarded person and very protective of proper appearances.

Nevertheless, I made a sojourn to my aunt's home, where I'd played as a child during family gatherings. Nostalgia gently passed through me as I mentally noted how unchanged the rural house and property were from my childhood days. I felt sad. My father accompanied me on my mission to lend me moral support.

As I visited with my aunt, I tried subtly to move the conversation to that night in 1955. Each time I did so a tense look crossed my aunt's face and I retreated, feeling guilty for pressuring an eighty-seven-year-old woman. I asked her whether I'd indicated to her what had frightened me on that night. She replied, "I think it was some kind of glow in the dark Lone Ranger mask on the wall, or something like that."

Performing a little mental arithmetic, I realized Jack had been twenty-four years old when I was three. He had returned from the Korean War, where he'd been wounded while serving in the Marine Corp. I seriously doubted he would have a childhood hero's mask on the wall. Was she trying to cover up her fear and suspicion that he'd hurt me, or did she sincerely not remember?

Trying a slightly different approach, I asked her about Jack's personality in general, carefully weaving in other unrelated conversation so that she might feel less threatened. We talked about how, at one point years before when my grandmother was staying with them,

Jack had said something to frighten my grandmother so severely that Grandmother telephoned my sister to come pick her up to protect her from Jack. Bess indicated she remembered the event but didn't elaborate from her storehouse of recollections.

Finally, I shared with Bess a scene described to me by my brother before Jack died, in which my brother had witnessed Jack threatening to kill Aunt Bess, his own mother. Her reaction was sudden and firm. She denied that such a scene had ever taken place, and I knew at that moment there was no future in discussing anything more. If she had information she wasn't about to share it with me, and furthermore, her commitment to truthfulness was tenuous. She was too threatened for me to challenge her further.

I was blocked from proceeding by the fact that I didn't have a clear memory that I could proclaim as truth. All I had were dreams and flashbacks. If I told her what I believed happened that night she would accuse me of lying, and I felt too fragile with my newly shed denial to take a risk. I visited the upstairs bedrooms before I left her house, and while I browsed I felt sad that I couldn't find a comfortable way to say what I had come so far, figuratively and literally, to say. I wanted information that might help me continue to heal, and I didn't want Aunt Bess to feel threatened or blamed in any way. I couldn't impart my message without doing so directly, and I judged that to be direct would bring a thick iron door down on our communication. A bit disheartened, I journeyed home.

Jack had been dead for nearly eleven years prior to my meeting with Aunt Bess. Protecting a long departed soul seemed ridiculous and unfair to me since to do so hampered the healing of the living. I wondered how I could reach her without her perceiving me as a threat. Perhaps my desire for things to be easy was the real problem.

Somewhat discouraged by my failure to acquire more clues to my mysterious past, I halfheartedly decided to explore one more avenue for self-discovery that didn't require the cooperation of anyone except me. I decided to enter hypnotherapy and I was fearful.

When I thought of hypnotherapy, I mentally compared the process of hypnosis with my labor to give birth to my first son. He was eleven days overdue and the labor process was a bit erratic. I was offered a drug, Pitocin, to stimulate labor and I refused to take it because I believed that if intense labor developed too rapidly, I would be little prepared and out of control, and rendered unable to manage natural childbirth. My fear of hypnosis was the same. I feared images would appear too abruptly and vividly for me to assimilate them in a useful manner. I inwardly argued with my fear, emphasizing to myself that I had survived the initial trauma in early childhood, and the flashbacks in adulthood. Surely, I reasoned, I could survive a few memories. I telephoned David Northway, a hypnotherapist with a strong positive local reputation and established an appointment time.

I remember during our first appointment a feeling of irritation for which I could determine no provocation. David was a tall, slender, soft-appearing man in his mid-forties, with full lips, expressive eyes, and receding gray curly hair. His voice was soft and deep. He seemed kind and interested in helping me. He collected a history and explained the limitations of hypnotherapy. He said he felt we should know whether or not the memories would be intact enough to retrieve within three to five sessions. And he asked me to think about how I would like the memories to come back. What form would I find most acceptable?

Although David was both kind and knowledgeable, I struggled to subdue my annoyance with him. Within a few nights of our first meeting I had an explanatory dream involving Edward. While the story line of the dream didn't survive the transition into waking consciousness, I realized upon awakening that my resentment of David was the product of my loyalty to Edward. My resentment had nothing whatsoever to do with David, only that he wasn't Edward. Having discovered the source of my annoyance, I easily gave it up and moved into the motions of getting to know David.

David was very gradual in his approach to hypnotherapy. His demeanor and style were neither pushy nor demanding. He offered a "little exercise" here and there to acclimate me to the induction of trance states. My sense of fearfulness diminished rather quickly.

On our fourth session, David inquired, again, as to the best way for me to receive the information I was seeking. I answered, "I've thought about your question and I think it would be best to come in the form of a dream. I don't want to have to struggle with intrusive images during my work through the day. I don't need a huge amount of emotion at this point, and it would be best if the dream isn't so convoluted that I can't make any sense of it." I was aware that I sounded as if I was placing an order at a fast food restaurant and felt slightly embarrassed at my demeanor of entitlement. Past experience had taught me that my unconscious was very clever at accessing nocturnal communication pathways. But I didn't want to sound impudent or disrespectful.

We proceeded to talk over the clues I already had, including that it happened in my aunt's upstairs bedroom at night. Ultimately I contacted emotions and openly wept the remainder of the session. Later that day, I made a journal entry:

It occurred to me the room might have been dark. David suggested smells, sound, and kinesthetic experience might be stronger than usual. Resistance kept asserting itself by way of anger, feeling the abuse was stupid and senseless. Then I felt the hand over my mouth and nose, and struggling to get my face free. Felt the rough, calloused, hot sweaty hands on my baby skin, pinching my face. Tears, tears. . .

That night I awoke from a dream at approximately 2:00 a.m. and made the following journal entry:

Dream: A small lamp is on in a bedroom with sloping ceilings. The light is dim. Someone is about to sodomize my son, Garrett, who I think is three.[1] The person positions Garrett with his tiny white buttocks sticking up, his knees beneath him. The light reflects off his pale skin and his little bottom appears to be the only thing in the room. The person presses forward to enter him. Garrett is sleeping, barely awake, and has no awareness of what is about to happen to him. I can see but I'm the omniscient narrator of the dream, not physically present, and I can't stop the event from happening. I am completely horrified. Overwhelmed by my emotional distress, I wake up.

Pulling myself out of my shock from the intensity of the dream, catching my breath, I couldn't help but marvel at how responsive my dream was to my request. The dream wasn't in any way convoluted or irrational. It was a simple portrayal of what had happened that night, thirty-seven years ago. The only difference was that my observing ego had judged the little child in the dream to be my son and not me, allowing me to preserve my adult perspective.

I had never considered the possibility that my abuse had involved sodomy, although from reading about child sexual abuse I was aware that sodomy is often the method of penetration when the child is too small to effect vaginal penetration. I was intensely aware of the absolute defenseless vulnerability of the victim in the dream, which triggered my own disbelief, confusion, and anger. What possible gratification could my cousin have achieved by anally raping a sleeping child? I still found it difficult to integrate the child as me. From the parental perspective of me as dreamer I could fully comprehend the perversity, sickness, and utter cruelty of the act. I could understand why sexual acts such as this are so difficult and painful for families to think about, let alone openly discuss.

I somehow allowed the dream to slip into the background of my awareness until the following weekend, which was Easter. Another reunion transpired and I was content to enjoy the company of my extended family, feeling in my heart that I was beginning to truly let the past be the past. Paradoxically, the more concrete my knowledge became, the less preoccupying I found it to be.

I volunteered to drive my mother home to her retirement facility following the reunion, and I realized it was the first time I had been alone with her since my return to the Northwest. I had deliberately kept her uninformed of my struggle with the abuse issue simply due to my belief that she would have nothing more to offer and it might upset her. She had suffered two small strokes in previous years that left her mildly impaired. I did not want to burden her without cause.

The conversation in the car reached a moment of pause when I unexpectedly dived into a confession of the abuse.

"Mom, I know you have an excellent memory and I have something I've been wanting to tell you but I've been afraid to because I didn't know how it might affect you. Remember when you telephoned me in Atlanta and told me that Jack had molested Linda?" I didn't wait for an answer." Well, he molested me, too. I've just been getting the memories back and I'm trying to learn everything I can that might help me."

She gasped and stiffened in her seat exclaiming, "Oh my God! He was a case. How did he get you by yourself?"

I proceeded to give her an abbreviated, simplified version of the sequence of events. She, in turn, proceeded to tell me what happened with Jack and my sister, in greater detail than she had ever given previously. Her voice was strong and spontaneous. Her thoughts, as she expressed them, were conveyed as though she was reliving the scene in the moment.

"Linda was sound asleep and I thought Jack was, too, when I got up to go to the train station to buy our tickets to go home. It wasn't even daylight when I left. When I got back to the hotel, Linda was crying, pacing up and down the street with Jack right behind her. I didn't figure out what had happened at first. I got back to the room and when I went to the suitcase my douche bag was laying on top of my clothes with shit on everything. I checked Linda and her bottom was all bloody. Oh...He was such a nut." She shook her head back and forth in disbelief with a look of despair on her face.

We pulled into her retirement home and her attention immediately turned to the routines of her nighttime preparation. The moment of contactful revelation was past. She had given me external confirmation of what my dream had already revealed. Never before had she told me what she suspected Jack had done to Linda, only that he had molested her. This was the first time I had any information suggesting sodomy. He'd been remarkably consistent across the ten years between his violation of my sister and me. He had awakened both of us from a sound sleep and sodomy had been his preferred method of violation. Another piece snapped into place. Once again, the message from my unconscious was supported by tangible evidence.

A week later I met with David and reported the interim events, amazed as I spoke by the precision and responsiveness of my own unconscious mind. He jokingly suggested that I should consider leaving psychology and redirect my talent for unconscious communication to the world of Wall Street where it might make me rich. We laughed, yet I was genuinely humbled by the mysterious accuracy that had been so great a part of my personal rediscovery process.

I explained to David that I had only two questions remaining. One was whether or not there had been more than one assault; the other was, if more than one assault occurred, was it always sodomy? David suggested a simple hypnotherapy technique in which I held my hands about six inches apart, a foot or so from my face. He posed the first question to me and suggested that if the answer was "yes," my fingers and hands would be attracted to each other. If the answer was "no," indicating only the one assault, my hands would be repelled from each other. I watched in careful anticipation as my fingers produced minute involuntary jerks toward the same fingers of the opposite hand. Finally, they touched, and David suggested I close my eyes and mentally observe any images that might come to my mind.

At first, nothing came to mind, and I enjoyed the momentary lack of thought for its relaxing meditative quality. Without conscious directive, I gradually felt a growing sense of having many people around, like a family reunion. I felt young and naive. I also felt that I was ignored by most of the adults. Nobody noticed me although I was dressed in a pretty dress and wore shiny black shoes with silver buckles. A grown-up, Jack, was leading me on a walk, away from the others. They were all talking and weren't noticing that we were going off by ourselves, alone. I felt special, but sad and scared. I sensed some woods and a barn, but the images changed from visual to kinesthetic and felt a streaming sensation from my pelvis down both legs. Not knowing for certain what happened, I was clear that this interaction with Jack had been more coercive and less brutal.

Coming out of the trance I felt a conviction that one of the episodes of molestation had taken place at a family gathering. David pointed out the irony that I was in a situation where all the adults who could have protected me were present, yet nobody did. I sometimes wonder if the other adults weren't pleased that Jack had taken me out so that I wouldn't be in the way of the adult activities. The thought saddens me. That night I dreamed the following:

In a kitchen a middle-aged woman is naked on the table and a doctor is at the foot of the table. He is going to do a pap smear and I am to hold her right leg. He tells me she is recovering from a rape of some time ago so I am to very careful and not upset her. I try to reassure them both of my sensitivity to their concerns, by telling them I, too, was raped as a child.

Dear Little Leia,

The reason I am writing to you is that I have something very important to tell you and I want you to listen very carefully. You are very little so you may not understand everything I am saying, but I want you to try as hard as you can.

I know you have been trying for a long, long time to tell me that someone hurt you. You have been very confused and sad. I made your sadness much worse when I didn't listen to you and when I tried not to believe what you were telling me. I am very sorry for not listening. I know now that you were telling me the truth; you never once told me a lie. I am proud of you for not lying and not giving up. I want you to know that I am very sorry for leaving you to hurt all alone.

You didn't deserve what Jack did to you. Nothing you did made it happen. You weren't bad and you didn't cause Jack to be mean to you. He just picked you to hurt because he had you alone to himself He would have hurt any child who was left alone with him. It wasn't your fault.

You deserve good things even though a bad thing happened to you. I still love you and other people still love you. Nobody thinks you are dirty or damaged. You are, and always will be, precious to me in every way. Your body is healed and healthy and you have nothing to be ashamed of.

I want you to know that I won't ever leave you again. I will listen to you and I will believe you when you have something to tell me. I hope you can forgive me for thinking that you lied. You must have been very lonely with your secret.

That is all I have to say for now.

Love,

Big Leia

Dear Big Leia,

I am happy that you believe me, and I am happy you don't think it was my fault. I didn't know why it happened. I thought maybe I was bad and that was why. But I didn't know what I did wrong so I was afraid I might do it again and be hurt again.

I still think my body is damaged sometimes but I'm glad you don't think so. I want you to love me.

I have stayed awake a long time to tell you what happened and to find out if it was my fault. Now that I know, I can go to sleep. I'm very tired. I want to sleep and dream about a white pony with wings that I can ride over clouds, and rainbow bubbles I can pop with my fingers. No one will wake me and hurt me now.

Love,

Little Leia

(This letter was written using the non-dominant hand.)

Dear Jack,

I have labored for months, now, trying to determine the best way to bring closure to my relationship with you. I have started letter after letter to you, only to realize that a few hours or days later my feelings have changed and the sentiments expressed on the pages no longer apply. The process of ending my relationship with you is like a condensed version of my struggle to heal from the trauma you bestowed on me, complete with rapidly changing emotions and abrupt shifts in my level of understanding of what happened. Trying to capture the essence of my feelings toward you has been like trying to contain a violent wind storm. I've decided, instead, to simply describe the damages resulting from your assault on me and tell you what I'm doing now to alter the legacy you left behind.

The first experience that comes to my mind that I believe resulted from you raping me is a pervasive feeling of fear that gripped me through much of my childhood. I often had terrifying nightmares and felt generally fearful in my waking hours as well. My sisters tell me that as a tiny child I often hid in a closet whenever visitors came to our home. I have vague memories of hiding, but I didn't understand the source of my fear so I couldn't obtain relief from others by talking or asking questions about it. In fact, your threat to kill me if I ever told was so firmly rooted in my unconscious mind that it literally became part of me, effectively silencing my waking mind from the truth, thereby preventing me from speaking of it. A sick part of you became sickness for me. In essence, I lost most of my childhood to the experience of torment and fear. I vacillated between despair and anguish hour by hour, day after day, not comprehending why, and possessing no method to undo the damage. I lost my physical innocence and purity to you, and in the process, my childhood was sacrificed. Teachers and family friends often described me as being old beyond my years, sullen, intense, and prematurely adult. I was robbed of my childhood. The childhood freedom from responsibility, to indulge in curiosity, and to engage in adventure was replaced by disturbed emotions I should not have been made to endure as a little child.

I have harbored the belief that there was something terribly wrong with me that I could do nothing to repair. I was freed of that misconception a few years ago when I learned the truth of our past—yours and mine. But I held that lie for thirty-five years, one-half of my life expectancy. Believing I was irreparably flawed, I have made choices throughout my life based on a feeling of inferiority to others. I allowed men to abuse me emotionally, and I secretly believed I deserved the mistreatment. I mistreated my own body through ingesting alcohol and drugs. I lived through several years of choosing sexual partners shallowly and indiscriminately, respecting neither them nor me. I hated myself for what I was doing and I believed I deserved no better. My self-hatred was like a pebble in a still pond, radiating outward in concentric circles adversely affecting others who risked coming into my life. I rejected truly loving people and sought companionship from others who were condemning, indifferent, or usurious of me. I believed I deserved rejection and criticism, although I didn't know why.

Whenever I received praise for success or positive recognition, I felt discomfort and guilt, sensing that I was unworthy of any successful loving human interactions. I didn't understand why I couldn't absorb positive input; I only knew that it made me more uncomfortable than punishment or suffering. I was at home with suffering; it was familiar to me from the tender age of three. Happiness and self-satisfaction resulting from genuine self-worth, these were the enemies because they threatened my unconscious belief that I deserved abuse, which was, for years, a safe prison cell built on the foundation of your violation of me. Worthlessness was my core identity and to change my identity was an illusory threat to my existence. I understand the illusion now, after years of enslavement by it. I knew who I was as a worthless person; I didn't know who or what I would be if I changed. For years I suffered, loathing myself as I was, and fearing who I might become if I changed. Change represented death to that which was familiar and predictable, and I tenaciously resisted change.

I protected the lie you imparted to me through your actions. I believed everything that you did to me was my fault and that I was a bad person. The belief that I was bad, I know now, was a clear and blatant lie. I couldn't let anyone know how bad I thought I was, and the safest way to keep the secret was for me to move my (perceived) badness into the deepest layers of my consciousness, where it could regulate my actions without being near enough to waking conscious awareness to risk disclosure.

I am appalled, now, when I consider the hideous outcome of the covenant, I entered into with you at a stage in my own development when alternative choices were outside my grasp. I forgive myself for not knowing what else to do at the time. I was three and I handled the trauma like a three-year-old, the very best, most obedient way I could. As bizarre as this may seem, I loved you and I didn't want to hurt you either. Jack, I am now to the point of breaking the covenant I made with you. I am telling the secret. I am rebuking the lies and misconceptions I developed. I am embracing my own goodness and sharing my true self without guilt or shame. I am freeing you to your own healing. Both the childhood and grownup aspect of me clearly realize the severity of the mental and emotional disturbance that plagued you throughout your lifetime, motivating you to acts of violence and perversity. While I still hold you, and you alone, responsible for your actions, I also forgive you, for the sake of both of us. I want freedom from you to complete my healing, and freedom for you to begin yours.

As I am ending this letter to you, I am ending my relationship with you. I wish you the peace that I claim for myself, and I hope that somehow our struggle for freedom from lies and pain may be transformed into a beacon to light the way for other perpetrators and victims in a march toward the wholeness we all deserve. Our mutual suffering will not, then, have been in vain.

In compassionate love,

Leia

Epilogue

Jack had died roughly eleven years prior to my learning of the violence he had perpetrated against me. The fact that it took me so many years to remember what I had experienced with Jack stands as proof for me that my unconscious mind is indeed benevolent. I was relatively shielded from the horrifying and painful memories until I reached an age at which I would be able to come to terms with them. As I worked through the process that has been described in these pages I pondered the meaning of the events from multiple perspectives. The most commonly applied meaning of such an event in our culture is that he was an evil person and I was an innocent victim. I was entirely innocent to be sure, but Jack was by no means purely evil. It isn't quite that simple.

A second perspective I pondered was the impact of Jack's deviant sexual behavior on Jack. His life and death were, by anybody's standards intolerably miserable. He died at age 51. I had not seen him since I was about 6 years old. According to his relatives, he had become grossly obese, socially isolated and intensely paranoid. I was told that for years he lived in fear of his home being broken into, and for that reason he kept a loaded shotgun by his front door to protect himself. When he died from a cardiovascular event, he was alone, and nobody mourned his passing.

It is a short step from one's personal guilt and shame for deliberately meting out injury to others to the fear of *being* injured, or retaliation. The human mind comes equipped with a strong built in tendency to keep score and identify patterns. Knowing that he perpetrated deviant and violent sexual acts toward my sister and me (and most probably uncounted others), on a conscious or unconscious level he must have anticipated there would someday be a reckoning and he would experience the consequences for what he had projected or perpetrated against others. The torment of living in constant fear of being discovered must have contributed to his living as a fugitive. He had to have considered what his fate might be if one of his child victims broke the silence and told a responsive, protective adult. So far as I know, nobody else came forward to disclose Jack's deviant behavior. Never the less, he knew what he had done. He knew he could be found out and what might happen if he was.

Jack eventually married and had one child, a son. He divorced his son's mother when the boy was less than two years old. Jack and his estranged wife fought for custody of the child for many years. The battle between Jack and his former wife was long and bitter on both sides. Jack's only son eventually grew into his young adulthood and became deeply involved with drugs and the legal system. Knowing that I was writing this book, a relative sent me a newspaper article reporting that Jack's son had raped an eleven-year-old girl and was scheduled to be sentenced to prison. I did not follow the progression of the story after that. I can say earnestly that the thread of pain that extended through Jack's family gave me no satisfaction. My healing was not served by any suffering of his family. Given that Jack was a pedophile, no doubt his son was influenced by Jack's nature if not one of Jack's victims.

In many ways the trauma Jack inflicted on me carried seeds of blessing. While I am clear that blessing, me was not at all Jack's purpose and I don't wish to imply that criminal violence is at all acceptable, I acknowledge that *ultimately,* I was not harmed by his actions. I eventually developed a deep level of compassion for others who had experienced childhood abuse of any kind. I learned to love myself and have compassion for the brave, injured child that is at the core of my character. As I progressed through the healing process I went on to experience meaningful relationships and to give birth to two sons who have blessed me beyond description through my years of rearing them to adulthood. I received a formal education and my passion for psychology may have been fueled by the struggle to find answers and heal from the wounds. My healing was facilitated along the way by extraordinary and loving people, therapists, family and friends. My body healed and released the memories of the abuse. I have no grudge left to bear.

The greater victim in this story was Jack. While he was never prosecuted for his actions, neither did he get away with anything. He constructed a hellish prison for himself that may have made real prison appear as a playground. He was described by his relatives as having been consumed with anger and his "heart attack" was no doubt as much a condition of the mind as of the body. However, his life and personal development can be viewed from another vantage point. By considering the larger context of his childhood environment, I can easily comprehend that he did not become who he was in a vacuum. His genetic inheritance, family culture and the greater culture at large produced the perfect storm to shape the character that he became. That does not excuse him. It does provide a framework from which to better understand who he was and why he did what he did. I needed a way to understand Jack that would move me beyond the bitterness of victimization. I needed to know that in his right-thinking mind, he would not have done what he did.

I am left with questions about the future. How will sexuality become reconnected with human loving? How will children be both free and safe to trust? My story is only one story among hundreds of thousands of such stories. I have no answers although I am profoundly optimistic that as truth comes to light and our culture is called to examine the conditions that give rise to dysfunction and trauma we will evolve and become better with identifying signs of sexually deviant behavior. Early intervention with intention to cultivate pro-social behaviors stands a chance of disrupting the patterns and cycles of abuse. My hope is that this story I have shared will raise awareness for the need to change attitudes and seek health in mind, body and spirit.

References

Bugental, J. (1990). Intimate journeys: Stories from life-changing therapy. San Francisco, CA: Jossey-Bass.

Smith, E. (2000). The body in psychotherapy. Jefferson, NC: McFarland & Company.

Smith, E. (1987). Sexual aliveness: A Reichian Gestalt perspective. Gouldsboro, ME: Gestalt Journal Press.

Yalom, I. (2012). Loves executioner. New York, NY: Basic Books.

Garrett was seven years old when this dream occurred.

www.ingramcontent.com/pod-product-compliance
Lightning Source LLC
Chambersburg PA
CBHW051224120626
46547CB00013B/1490